Memoirs of an Adoptee

ROOTED

LORI WILLIAMS

Rooted

Memoirs of an Adoptee

©2021, Lori Williams

ISBN: 978-1-66782-085-9

ISBN eBook: 978-1-66782-086-6

CONTENTS

CHAPTER 1:

Reflections from All Sides

It was a cold January evening in southeastern Wisconsin. I sat in my living room, glass of wine in hand, surrounded by an explosion of moving boxes and scattered housewares. My husband and I were newlyweds who had decided it would be brilliant to move in the middle of winter. Everything was in complete and utter disarray. So, naturally, I decided it was the perfect time to write a book.

I flopped down on the couch after a night of bubble wrapping and boxing our belongings. Sipping my wine, I allowed myself to survey the work I had just accomplished. My attention lingered on three beautiful mirrors leaning against our walls, waiting to be carefully packaged for the move. Each one had either been gifted to us or inherited from a family member over the years.

One was given to my maternal grandparents on their wedding day in 1946. It hung on the walls of their various homes throughout their lives. They were married on a cold January day, like the one I'd just spent packing up our condo. As their only grandchild, I was happy to inherit their beautiful mirror. Ever since I was a child, I had always admired its ornate golden frame surrounding the rectangular panel of beveled glass. It looked like something you might see in an old English manor. When my grandfather passed away in 2016, my mother took on the monumental task of going through all of his belongings. Many black and white snapshots from her childhood included the beautiful mirror in the background. It's a rich piece of family history that I will pass on to my own children one day.

My maternal grandparents, Jerry and Helen Gerg, were always a beacon of light and love in my life. Their relationship was like a romance plucked straight from the silver screen. Before they ever officially met, Helen used to sit on her porch on Sundays and watch Jerry drive past in his yellow sports car. Every week as she watched him go by, she would tell my great grandmother, "I'm going to marry that man."

One day, as fate would have it, she and my grandfather were at the local roller skating rink at the same time. She witnessed him drop a penny near the edge of the rink and she skated over to pick it up. At this point, she and Jerry had still not yet been formally introduced. Instead of giving the coin back to him, she took that penny home, drilled a hole in it, and wore it around her ankle for good luck. A few weeks later, their paths crossed again and my grandfather asked her out on their first date, a stroll by the local lake. Soon, they made a habit of sitting by the lake eating Cracker Jack together. Several months went by, and the United States entered World War II. Grandpa Jerry enlisted with the air force and he and Helen agreed to stay in touch, but he told her not to wait for him if she found a beau she wanted to marry. He didn't want her putting her life on hold for him. That's just the kind of man he was, always putting others before himself. They wrote each other letters the entire time that my grandfather was away at war. My grandmother went on an occasional date here or there, but her heart was always with Jerry.

Grandpa Jerry's time serving in World War II as a B-25 bomber pilot was not without struggles. One particular incident that he experienced could have cost him and his flight crew their lives. He was twenty-two years old on the day that he played a hand in saving his fellow crew members from what was intended to be a fatal event. The Allied forces were making substantial progress toward pushing the Nazis out of Naples, Italy. In order to stop the

Allies from progressing further, the Nazis were planning to drag a large barge across a major shipping port. On June 22, 1944, the mission of the Allies was to sink the barge before it could be positioned across the entrance of the bay. When my mother spoke with my grandfather decades after the event, Jerry painfully recalled,

> *"The anti-aircraft flak was saturating the sky. All six planes in our group were taking heavy hits, but they did not abort. We were successful at sinking the barge, still tied up at the breakwater, leaving the entrance to the bay open and usable by our Allied shipping. It was a very costly mission. Out of my box of six planes, only two returned. I saw four planes go down behind us. Of those four planes, a total of twenty-four men, I only saw one man parachute out."*

Jerry's plane was severely damaged, and the pilot was seriously injured. There was only one functional engine and the hydraulics and back-up hydraulics were completely shot out, leaving no flaps, no wheels, and a gaping hole where the hand crank used to be. Even though they were injured themselves, possessing only one usable arm and leg between the two of them, Jerry and his pilot maneuvered their crippled bomber back to safety, just feet above the Mediterranean Sea. The sea's waves splashed up on the plane's windshield as they struggled to maintain altitude. Just in the nick of time, the plane landed on solid ground on its belly, with gasoline spewing out and sparks flying. Miraculously, it didn't go up in flames until every last man was safely out. The lives of all seven people on Jerry's plane were saved that day. He received the Distinguished Flying Cross and the Air Medal, and his unit received a Presidential Unit Citation.

After the war, Helen was still waiting at home for Jerry. Following his life-altering brush with death, he returned ready to propose to her. One afternoon, he picked her up in his yellow car and they drove down to their spot at the lake to catch up and eat Cracker Jack. That day, however, he had hidden her engagement ring inside of the Cracker Jack box. When she found the ring instead of a chintzy prize, Jerry proposed. Of course, Helen said yes. Jerry and Helen were married for nearly sixty wonderful years. Their example of commitment to each other and their family is the reason I believe in true love.

In January of 2018, it was seventy-two years to the day of their wedding anniversary as I gazed at their mirror sitting in my living room. I thought of their legacy of love and thanked God for the memories I made with them over the years.

Across the room from Jerry and Helen's mirror, another mirror hung on the wall of our condo. It was a large oval surrounded by a golden floral frame, ornately lovely. It always reminded me of the magic mirror in the fairy tale *Snow White*. I inherited it from my paternal grandparents in 2017, after my grandmother's passing. When I was a child, I used to stand in front of it and pretend it was magic, playing a game of *"Mirror, Mirror on the Wall..."* My paternal grandparents, Al and Bette Engelmeier, both had a great sense of humor and they would always play along whenever they caught me in my pretend games. Their love story is a true wartime romance.

World War II had already begun, and like many women her age, Bette went to nursing school in hopes of using her skills to help soldiers in need. It was the night of her graduation, and her nursing school class went out on the town to celebrate their accomplishments. Al Engelmeier's military regiment happened to be on leave at the same time, and the boys in uniform crowded the club where my grandmother and her classmates were celebrating. Bette wasn't even of legal drinking age yet and had to fib her way into the place. Already uneasy about standing out as the baby of the bunch, she was even more unsettled when a tall, dark, and handsome man in uniform approached her group of friends, singling her out and asking her to dance. Al and Bette danced the night away and agreed to spend more time together in the following days of Al's leave. The days flew by and their infatuation with each other grew. Al was set to ship out to Nova Scotia after his basic training and couldn't bear the thought of living without Bette to come home to. After only three dates, in a fit of wartime romance, he proposed. Two weeks later, Bette found herself on a train to Fort Benning, Georgia, a beautiful bride to be! They were married on the base and Al left for Nova Scotia two days later. Their marriage lasted over sixty years. They never left each other's side through thick and thin, just like my mother's parents. My grandparents were shining role models of what a strong, committed, and loving marriage should look like.

As I gazed at both of the mirrors in my living room, my thoughts spiraled into the symbolism of the reflection staring back at me. I am a conglomeration of the people who have shaped my life, mixed with my own unique traits. A person's identity is not primarily a question of nature or nurture. It is a consortium of both.

When we look in the mirror, we see who we are, but it's an inverted image. We rely on what we know of ourselves to guide what we see in our reflection, all the while knowing that we are much, *much* more than meets the eye. Growing up as an adopted child is similar to looking into that mirror, like holding onto a Polaroid picture of your reflection, without ever having looked into the mirror itself.

In a way, these family heirloom mirrors not only represented my identity, but also the past, present, and future. As a child, my past was a beautiful mystery to me. I received photos and letters from the semi-open adoption arrangement that my parents had made, but I never met my birth parents. I looked at those photos of my biological parents and wanted so desperately to find a piece of myself staring back at me. As an adult, I went on to reconnect with both of my birth parents in different ways. I never dreamed that I would see my birth family and the family that raised me come full circle through the catalyst of my wedding, but I was blessed to witness this take place. The work I did in my twenties to make sense of all of my familial relationships is what made that possible, in conjunction with the open-mindedness of all of the parties involved.

When I look at my reflection today, the future holds promise. Gone is the yearning found in the mirror of my past, searching for oneness in the missing fragments. As I share my story with you, I hope to reflect back the challenges, joy, and love of three families who made me who I am today.

CHAPTER 2:

❦

"So, Who's Your Birth Mom?"

BEFORE I LAUNCH INTO TELLING you my story, I want to clarify some details. My mom is my mom. She will always be my mom. The woman who raised me will always be the woman I refer to as Mom, so when I describe my mother, this is the woman to whom I am referring. At differing times throughout my story, I also refer to the parents who raised me as my adoptive parents. This is simply for the sake of clarity. My parents are my parents. The people who brought me into this world, physically, I refer to throughout my writing as my birth parents or biological (bio) parents. Now that we have that out of the way, let's dive in …

From the time I was young, I was well aware of my identity as an adopted person. I knew where I came from as simply as a child knows night from day. My parents did a fantastic job of normalizing my situation for me. Mine was a semi-open adoption. My birth parents sent letters and pictures through a social service and my adoptive parents did the same. From the time I could talk, my mother happily read me the letters and shared every picture sent to us by Adrienne and Todd, my birth parents. She explained how young they were when I was born. They were hardly more than children themselves at sixteen and seventeen years old. She read letters in which they described their interests and hobbies, and how much they loved me, and how they wished the world for me and for my adoptive parents. It was almost like having two very special pen pals … a mother and father figure whom I had known but did not remember. Until I started to attend school, I was under the impression that all families were just like mine. I remember the precise moment of my childhood when I learned that this was not the case.

One day during preschool, I approached my friend, Becca, and casually asked her who her birth mother was. She looked at me blankly, as if I were speaking a foreign language. On that particular day, she and I were also having a play date after school. When my mom picked us up, I remember telling her how concerned I was that my friend didn't know who her birth mother was. *Surely,* I thought, *this was a mistake, and my mother could help us remedy the situation.* My mom explained to me that Becca's mom was her birth mother. I was dumbfounded. When we dropped Becca off at the end of our playmate, I asked her mom if she was indeed, her birth mother. Sure enough, when I asked her, she confirmed what my mother had told me, and I distinctly remember how it absolutely blew my mind. From that moment on, I realized that I had a unique identity as an adopted person.

The following school year, I started kindergarten at Holy Name of Jesus Elementary School in Wausau, Wisconsin. There were about fifteen students in my class, most of them from very traditional Northern Wisconsin families. The first week of school, us wee kindergarteners were greeted by a gloriously decorated bulletin board near the entrance of the classroom, filled with fun facts and photos featuring my teacher, Mrs. Kay. Mrs. Kay started off the school day with a riveting presentation, describing the bulletin board as the Star-of-the-Week display. Since she was the Star of the Week, Mrs. Kay described the artifacts on the bulletin board in great detail. We were all interested to hear about her family, hobbies, and her favorite TV show. The experience of learning this kind of in-depth personal information about our kindergarten teacher was beyond exciting for a classroom full of curious five year olds. After she wrapped it up by taking a few rapid-fire questions from the crowd, Mrs. Kay told us that each child in the class would have their own opportunity to be Star of the Week. One day, it would be our very own turn to bring the bulletin board to life with the details of our own lives! It was Mrs. Kay's way of helping all the new kindergarteners feel at home in her classroom.

When it was my long-awaited turn, I brought in photos of my family along with some of the birth parents I only knew through letters and pictures. I showed off my dog, Buddi, a picture of myself in my Halloween costume from the previous year, another from a dance recital, and a few of my parents and I, snapped during happy days spent outside in the Wisconsin Northwoods. The pictures I hung of Adrienne and Todd were from their senior year of high school, proudly displayed alongside all the rest. Mrs. Kay helped me explain to the class that I was adopted. Most of the students had never heard of adoption or considered that such a thing existed in the world. My Star-of-the-Week performance was quickly derailed and turned into an interrogation led by well-meaning but prodding five year olds.

"Why didn't your mom and dad want you?"

"So you were an orphan?"

"Don't you miss your real mom?"

"Do you think your real mom and dad miss you?"

"Will you ever go back to your real mom and dad someday?"

Um, *ouch.*

I felt ostracized and hurt that my classmates would say these things to me. I was confused and sad by their intrusiveness. They had brought up issues I had never even considered before. Sensing how overwhelmed I was, Mrs. Kay stepped in.

"All right, that will be enough questions, everyone. Lori is very lucky to have two sets of special grownups who love her. If she wants to tell you more, she will, but it's up to her. No more questions for today."

The kids dropped the issue entirely by recess time, but I was left to think about all that had transpired. At the tender age of five, I was already grappling with the existential questions of my identity.

I never told my mom about the Star-of-the-Week incident, but she sensed what was happening in my life. Even though she and I had a very close and open relationship, I never directly shared my new feelings with her. This was because I felt guilty for even having them. It was the first time in my life that my identity as an adopted person made me feel sad. It made me feel different. My classmates had opened doors I had never even known existed. I never considered my birth parents to be my real parents. My mom and dad were my mom and dad! How dare my peers suggest otherwise? The sudden barrage of questioning from my classmates allowed doubts to creep into my young mind. Were my adoptive parents really my parents? Did my peers know something I didn't know about the natural order of family life? Was I a weirdo because the mother who was raising me wasn't the mother who gave me life? Should I feel a certain level of absence in my life because my birth parents weren't physically in it? And the biggest question of all … was it a betrayal to my parents that I suddenly had all these questions about my birth parents and my identity?

When I turned six in October, I found myself feeling very sad. With all of the new questions swirling around in my little mind, I was beginning to know inner turmoil as I never had before. October fourteenth rolled around, and there I was wondering where my birth parents were. I wondered if they knew that it was my birthday and if they were thinking of me. I let myself wonder why they didn't want to keep me and if I could ever go back to them if I wanted to. When I asked my mother some of these questions, she reassured me that I had nothing to worry about. She told me that my birth parents loved me so much that they had to give me a better life than they could provide. They were simply too young, they weren't married, and they couldn't have supported a healthy home for a child. She told me that for her and my father, who couldn't have children of their own, I was a precious gift. She told me that no matter what happened, she was my mom and she would always take care of me.

"You're telling me they loved me so much they didn't want to keep me? That makes no sense!!" I tried to accept this as truth from my tenderhearted mother, even though I couldn't understand it. For many years after my fateful Star-of-the-Week presentation, my birthday always brought with it the same feelings of melancholy and unanswered questions.

Little did I know that before I was even born, my birth parents had hand-sifted through numerous adoption applicants at Lutheran Social Services to place me with the right couple. There were many reasons why they chose Rick and Pam Engelmeier. My mother exudes kindness from every pore of her being, and my father is calm and competent in all things. My father is extremely intelligent and hardworking, with a kind heart and a quick sense of humor. My mother is the sweetest and most genuine person you could ever hope to meet. My father's care and concern for others was evident in his many years of private practice as a cardiologist. My mother worked as a physical therapist helping veterans and the elderly, and still volunteers for an equine therapy program serving the disabled and people struggling with mental illness. Adrienne and Todd could not have picked a better couple to raise me.

While I was growing up, my parents provided a balance of strict rules and logical discipline along with warmth and encouragement. They bent over backward to ensure that I lived a full and well-rounded life. I know that part of Adrienne and Todd's decision to place me with the Engelmeiers was due to their healthy lifestyle and love of the outdoors. My parents provided me with a loving home as well as abundant opportunities for fun and growth. We took frequent trips to our family lake house, camping trips to national parks, vacations exploring the globe ... and there were dance lessons, ice skating lessons, gymnastics, swimming lessons, piano lessons, violin lessons, horse camp, and countless other extracurricular activities. To an outsider looking in, I had the best of all worlds. I knew this, and it only enhanced my feelings of guilt for wondering about my birth parents and feeling a sense of incompleteness. I never addressed my feelings with my parents. Instead, I held them inside for years, ashamed of feeling them. Eventually, they caught up with me. No matter where you go, there you are.

CHAPTER 3:

⤙⤙⤙

Dancing Dreams Come True

As I GREW OLDER, I definitely gave my parents a run for their money. Like most teenagers, I went through a rebellious phase. They tried their best, but I often think that my parents didn't quite know what to do with their occasionally partying, sometimes cigarette-smoking, boy-crazy, and rebellious teenage daughter. Adolescence is a time of identity crisis and development for all teens, and this journey is only further complicated as an adoptee. At least in most homes, parents see a streak of themselves in their teen's rebellion and can manage it better because of it. My parents truly couldn't relate to my behavior at all.

In their youth, my parents were well-behaved, straight-laced, straight-A teenagers. In my teen years, I kept up with grades and extracurricular activities, but I also dabbled in the experimentation of teen partying with some of my peers. Later, I would find out that my birth father was the same way in his youth. In Wisconsin, it is not at all uncommon for teenagers to attend drinking parties, especially out in the countryside where parents go so far as to collect car keys, supply beer, and make sure that no one leaves for the night. I didn't set out to be a rebel. I just went along with the crowd and I enjoyed having a good time. I think it would have been infinitely easier on my parents and myself if they were able to see a piece of themselves in my behavior, as my birth father would have. They governed with zero-tolerance rules, which only caused me to rebel more strongly.

My high school clique would often listen to tales of my adventures with amusement, and a few days later, my mom would receive a phone call reporting my weekend escapades. I never found out who it was that decided to report my every action to their mother, who then reported it to mine. Their teenage life must have been pretty dull if the high point of it was gossiping with their mom.

It was this kind of petty nonsense that made me feel like an outsider. My friends were all very conservative and well-behaved, and I was the party girl who did what she wanted on the weekend, running with the good girls during the school week. My party friends were a separate group from my school clique, and my school clique knew it. I was also different in that I was an artistic personality while everyone in my small-town high school was more focused on sports and 4-H. I was a ballet dancer all my life and planned to pursue it as a career. I chalked up my somewhat negative high school experience to having different interests than my peers. I felt more at home in the dance studio than anyplace else in the world. Dance has always allowed me to express myself and be free in ways I can't in my everyday life. I just knew that being accepted into a reputable college dance degree program would finally help me find where I fit in the world.

My senior year of high school, 2008, was spent attending college dance program auditions and rehearsing for my youth ballet company's production of *The Little Mermaid*. It was also the year that my company celebrated ten years of bringing ballet to the masses in north central Wisconsin. I was performing the title role in our production and it was my ultimate dream come true. My company director, Mrs. Dean, had performed with the American Ballet Theater in New York City in her youth. She used her connections to bring two of the country's best ballet dancers from this prestigious company to Wausau, Wisconsin, to perform as part of our Decade of Dance celebration. Julie Kent and her ballet partner Marcelo Gomes performed a *pas de deux* from Swan Lake just before the intermission of our show. Both were principal dancers with the American Ballet Theatre at the time. They are some of the most successful and highly praised dancers in the industry. It was breathtaking watching them warm up before the show and then witnessing them perform from the wings backstage. As a young girl with big aspirations, it was absolutely surreal for me.

A performance of this magnitude garnered a lot of press, especially in a town the size of Wausau. The presence of Julie Kent and Marcelo Gomes on the program brought in dance fans from all over the state and the greater Midwest. People who had never been interested in ballet before recognized the opportunity to see world-class dancers from New York City and came to the theater in droves.

On the show's closing night, I was celebrating backstage with the other cast members. I was riding high from the magnitude of performing my dream role, socializing with two of my ballet idols, and watching them dance from such close proximity. It seemed as though a million people were laughing, hugging, and celebrating behind the curtain. In the midst of all the revelry, a slender woman who looked to be in her fifties with a pixie haircut and a warm smile approached me.

"Hello, Lori," she said, her eyes sparkling.

I knew I had seen her face before, but I couldn't place where. I assumed she must have been one of my mother's church friends who all seemed to know my life story, yet whose first names I could barely keep track of.

Caught up in the excitement of the moment, I said hello and embraced her in a warm hug. Then she identified herself and I was a little mortified for being so overly friendly. Seemingly out of thin air, she produced a business card with her name and title on it. Then she said, "Congratulations on an outstanding performance, Lori. As director of the University of Wisconsin-Stevens Point Dance Department, I'd like to formally welcome you to our program for fall of 2008, assuming you'll accept your place."

I was completely dumbfounded. My dance dreams had all come true over the course of a single weekend.

"Yes, yes, of course! Oh my gosh, thank you so much!" We exchanged a few words and then she said, "You have some celebrating to do and I'll leave you to it. Congratulations again, and we'll see you in the fall!"

Unbeknownst to me, another dream was unfolding in the audience while I was onstage. My birth father, Todd Kurth, and his wife, Jamie, brought their two little girls to see *The Little Mermaid*. The Kurths lived an hour away in Minocqua, Wisconsin, and came to town for the performance because they recognized what a unique opportunity it was, especially for the girls. They were shocked when, upon their arrival at the theater, they saw my name headlining the program.

I was unaware of their attendance at the show until I received a letter a few weeks later. Todd had taken the time to send it after years of silence on his end. It read,

Dear Lori,

I know it has been years since I have written and for that, I am truly sorry. I always thought of you, but never knew what to say, and I didn't want to interfere in your life. Last weekend, I took my daughters to see *The Little Mermaid*' at the Grand Theater in Wausau. I was completely in awe as I watched you dance onstage. You have grown up to be a beautiful, graceful, and talented young woman.

I've enclosed a photo of me taken on a snowmobile outing a few years back. My wife, Jamie, took the photo, and I had intended to send it to you. Like I said, I always wanted to write to you, but didn't know what to say. Jamie told me, "If you don't write to her, you are breaking a little girl's heart." I know that many years have passed since I last wrote to you, and I am sincerely sorry if you feel that way.

Watching your performance was incredible for all of us. Please know that if you want to contact us at any time, our door is always open. You have two sisters who would love to meet you one day.

Love,
Your birth father, Todd Kurth

I was surprised to say the least. It was a lot to digest after having just experienced so many momentous events in my life. After my initial reaction passed, I thought, *What right does this man have to my attention now?* I really didn't know much about my birth father at this point, except that he was no longer with my birth mother. The revelation of two sisters who not only knew about me but also wanted to meet me was an additional shock.

The letter arrived in late spring of 2008. I was busy working and preparing for college. I was looking forward to diving into that experience headfirst and I didn't want anything or anyone standing in my way. I knew I would irreversibly open a door I wasn't yet ready to enter if I responded to Todd's letter. So, I let it be and I tucked it away in a drawer for someday.

Someday, I thought, *I'll be ready. Today is not that day.*

CHAPTER 4:

※

College Days

AWAY FROM MY PARENTS AND finding my feet, I was trying hard to establish my new identity. Even though I was exactly where I wanted to be, I still experienced the gnawing feeling that a piece of me was missing. I continued to feel as though I didn't really fit anywhere.

In the university dance program, the people I danced with as well as the instructors were all very pretentious and self-important. The world of dance is competitive. The fact that my classmates and I were in the dance program meant that we had already beat out dozens of other dancers to earn our spots. Many dancers and artistic performers see their peers as adversaries to overcome if they are to succeed. This attitude exists everywhere in the professional dance world. It trickles down from places like Julliard, all the way to the small dance studios of the Midwest. This type of mentality was rampant among the college classmates I spent my days with. It cast a hard edge to almost everyone in the dance program and left me feeling like I couldn't trust anyone. I received an anonymous piece of hate mail during my first semester of college that had obviously been written by a dance classmate, as it expressed knowledge only someone in the dance program would know. This definitely set the tone for the rest of my college dance career by showing me I had to be in it to win it, not to make friends.

It was my first real taste of the professional dance world, a sort of microcosm of dance-company life. Before it all began, I had always thought I'd move from university dance life to New York City, Chicago, or another metropolis and begin my career as a professional dancer. That dream changed swiftly once I entered the program. The cliques and drama of the small pond of the university were enough to open my eyes to reality. I felt that being a part of the Theater and Dance program at the university was unlike anything else. Grading really just came down to favorites. The suck-ups and teacher pleasers would get all the good roles and perfect grades, while those who challenged the status quo didn't get cast as frequently or for as many major roles, regardless of technical dance ability or dedication. I worked hard in the dance program and respected my peers and teachers, but I refused to worship the ground they walked on. This ultimately worked against me, but I graduated proudly and never looked back at the people I left behind. I have exactly one friend from the college dance program whom I have remained close to.

The woman who showed up backstage at my performance during my senior year of high school was the worst of all. Karen ran the dance department like its own little kingdom designed to serve her. She was vicious and she enjoyed it. She was a bully and she liked making people squirm. Her whole M.O. was to push students to their breaking point just to see if they'd stick it out or quit. The class ahead of mine lost half of their roster by sophomore year. She would say and do the most outrageous things, things that I'm sure in today's climate of political correctness would have gotten her reprimanded or fired. But this was more than a decade ago, and the dance world was beholden only to itself. She held the kingdom's keys.

One day, in jazz class, we were performing a sexy Fosse routine. The Fosse technique of jazz is highly sensual. A girl by the name of Melissa, who was devoutly Christian, was struggling with the blunt sexuality of the choreography. She had a nervous habit of bringing her fingers to the cross she wore around her neck. Karen noticed this, and she got right up in Melissa's face and said in front of the whole class, "Take off that crucifix and dance already."

Another girl in the program was the most talented dancer in my small hometown of Wausau, Wisconsin. She had the technicality and precision to execute any routine flawlessly and her style matched her ability. Although she trumped us all with her flawless triple pirouettes and leg extensions that reached her forehead, she wasn't built "like a dancer." Anna had an ass. And the thighs to go with it. As she made her way through college, her figure expanded more and more. Her dancing never suffered, but her body didn't fit the ballerina aesthetic. During her second year in the program, she had a one-on-one academic advising meeting with Karen that ended with Karen telling her, "You know, you could go far if you'd watch your figure more. Maybe you should just eat some almonds or an orange for lunch instead of an entire sandwich." Anna left the meeting in tears.

Aside from dance, another medium of self-expression I delved into during my college years was modeling. I became deeply involved in the modeling scene and I started booking photo shoots every weekend. Most of my work took me to Milwaukee, Wisconsin, but the farthest I traveled for work was Las Vegas. I felt that my success as a model would bring me the happiness and sense of completeness I longed for, but of course, it didn't. It left me feeling burned out and more insecure than I had before. There's never an end to the work it takes to keep your skin, hair, and figure top-notch as a model. You win some, you lose some, and you go half crazy trying to be better than the girl next to you, who could easily slide into your stilettos and take your job in a heartbeat. It was not a lifestyle that was healthy for me.

I made it through all four years of the dance program because I saw it as a challenge I had to tackle. Karen was not going to break me or beat me down to the point that I didn't love dance anymore. The biggest test of my determination came during a choreography project my senior year. I had dedicated the piece to my mother, who was going through her second battle with breast cancer in only two years. My mother and I are extremely close and it was a trying time for both of us. I created the piece as a way to show my support for her and as an outlet of expression for myself. One day in class, all of us dance majors were sharing the topics of our work and why we had chosen our themes. When it was my turn, I explained that the work

I was creating was a means for me to support my mother's journey through her cancer treatment.

In front of the entire class, Karen responded with, "That's nice. But really, aren't you afraid that your mother is dying? Isn't that what you want to express?"

It sucked the air right out of me. The tears of fear I'd been holding back through all of my mother's treatments came cascading down my face in front of fifteen of my peers who were just as taken aback as I was. You could have heard a pin drop in the room. The woman enjoyed creating chaos for a reaction and watching people hit their rock bottom. And yet, my peers willingly bent over backward to grant her wishes and kissed her behind night and day in hopes of getting some trivial role or a better spot at the barré. It was ludicrous. No wonder I felt that I couldn't trust anyone.

I honestly thought that college would be the cure-all for the small town nonsense and pointless drama of high school. I assumed that my admission into the fancy dance program would fill the void and put to rest the questions I had about myself, but I was disappointed when I was about to graduate and I realized that college hadn't magically shown me who I was. As I learned, the characters in the dance program bore a startling resemblance to the cast of the movie *Mean Girls*, but with bun heads and ballet shoes.

The everyone-for-themselves mentality of the dance department caused me to seek relationships outside of my day-to-day peer group. It was a necessity if I wanted to keep my sanity. I was longing to meet someone genuine and trustworthy. At the end of my freshman year of college with the bitchy ballerinas from hell, I met a boy named Carter. Carter was older than me and he was also a member of the Theater and Dance department. He was an acting major, and he had aspirations of moving to Los Angeles after college. He shared with me once that he had a director friend who lived in Los Angeles who had roles waiting for him as soon as he could move out to the West Coast and start working. He was an attractive and funny guy and also a bit of an outsider, by choice. He had his own ideas and opinions and he didn't cast those aside for anyone, even when his directors demanded it or his peers didn't agree with him. This earned him a certain level of respect in the department, although he was more infamous than appreciated for his authenticity. He lured me quickly into his aura of quirky romance and I fell hard. It was us against the world for about a year. In that time, I became entranced. I thought my relationship with the older, cooler actor made me strong and independent, but it didn't. Not at all.

I was very dependent on a very toxic person. The worst point in my relationship with Carter came in December of 2010 when he became physically abusive. A small fight had turned major, as it often did with Carter's volatile personality, and it ended with him trying to smother me with a pillow. I remember the room starting to go black as I struggled to breathe. Something in me found the strength to fight him off. My autonomic nervous system went into overdrive and I threw off the pillow and all six-foot-three inches of him, slamming him into a nearby dresser. I grabbed my things and ran out the door.

Although I walked away that night, Carter found a way to sweet talk his way back into my life. It was the classic cycle of abuse and forgiveness that is the hallmark of many unhealthy relationships. I had wrapped my identity around my relationship with him so fully that I didn't know how to walk away permanently, even though I knew it was wrong for me to stay. I was smart enough and strong enough to know that I deserved better, yet I was afraid to start again, picking up the pieces of something I was naïve enough to believe would last forever.

On December 24, 2010, my life irreversibly changed. I was given an incredible Christmas gift that propelled me forward with the strength to start over and walk into a new chapter of my life. At twenty-one years old, God decided I was ready to take the plunge and He pushed me off the deep end into my Christmas miracle.

CHAPTER 5:

The Magic of Christmas Eve

CHRISTMAS EVE OF 2010 WAS slightly out of the ordinary. Usually, my family traveled from Wausau to Milwaukee, Wisconsin, to spend Christmas with my dad's side of the family. My three sets of aunts and uncles, paternal grandparents, and my cousins are all from the Milwaukee suburbs. For this reason, we spent pretty much every holiday in the Milwaukee area. My mother, like me, was an only child, and we usually celebrated with her dad after the family events in Milwaukee were over. This particular year, we had decided to switch things up a bit by going to Minocqua, Wisconsin, to attend church. Grandpa Jerry, my mom's dad, was living alone in the Northwoods at the time. Once in a while, he would travel with us to Milwaukee, but he was getting on in years and it was harder and harder for him to make the trip. In 2010, we decided to see him on Christmas Eve and celebrate with the other side of the family at a later date.

We prepared our Christmas meal and ate at my grandfather's house. After dinner, we moved to the living room where my grandparents' mirror hung on the wall, reflecting back our Christmas fellowship. This was the mirror I would later inherit, the one my grandparents received as a wedding gift in 1946.

I don't remember much about that Christmas Eve because my heart and mind were still so twisted up with the trauma I had experienced at the hands of Carter. I hadn't told anyone about the violent incident between us. I was trying to face it on my own. I was very distracted throughout the night.

The time came for us to get ready for church. We bundled up to keep out the single-digit wind chill and piled into the car to head over to the Christmas Eve church service. We arrived at the entrance of the small Lutheran church and were greeted by two ushers handing out programs. The ushers were a man and woman who looked to be in their late thirties. As the man standing there handed me my program, the expression on his face looked like he had just seen a ghost. It was odd, but I took my seat with my family and tried not to think anything of it. I figured I must have been imagining things since I was not in a good place mentally to begin with.

Throughout the service, I noticed the acolyte staring at me. She was a pretty brunette girl who looked to be about eleven or twelve years old. At many different points throughout the evening, I noticed her eyes were directly fixed on me. I thought it must have been in my head. *First the usher, now the acolyte? I must be going crazy after everything with Carter.* Halfway through the service, I walked up for communion, and when her eyes followed me all the way down the aisle and back to my pew, I knew something was happening. I couldn't put my finger on what it was, but I knew that it was a little eerie. I was truly starting to get a little freaked out.

Several months earlier, a girl named Brianna Kurth had sought me out by finding my profile on social media. She contacted me through private messaging, explaining that she was my twelve-year-old half-sister and that she would like to meet me one day. She told me about herself, her interests, and her life in the small town of Minocqua, Wisconsin, where she lived with her sister, Morgan, and, of course, my birth father, Todd, and his wife. She went on to say that they were all excited to meet me one day. I was a bit taken aback by the sudden communication from someone I had never before dreamed of meeting. I was working as a counselor at a summer camp when Brianna reached out to me, and I didn't have the free time to get away to meet her that summer. I wasn't even completely sure that I was willing to. I knew that meeting her would break open a whole new world, and that was frightening to me. So, my job became the perfect excuse to put off the meeting for the whole summer and wait for her to reach out again once the summer had passed.

God had other plans, which were set into motion on that fateful Christmas Eve. That acolyte in the church who wouldn't stop staring at me? That was my half-sister, Brianna. That usher who looked like he had seen a ghost? That was my birth father, Todd. He and his wife, Jamie, were handing out programs that night. He had known the moment we walked in the door who we were. My parents didn't recognize him, as he no longer looked like the mullet-headed teenager they knew twenty-one years before. I didn't recognize Brianna because we had never exchanged pictures, only messages. But there it was, loud and clear. A Christmas miracle so in-my-face I couldn't ignore it if I tried.

The moment I realized what was happening, I felt like I was living in a dream. It was as if those moments were happening to someone else. Everything took on a hazy, slow-motion quality, yet my brain raced a million miles a minute. The lights were turned off in the Sanctuary and the church was entirely illuminated by candles. The acolytes moved throughout the congregation pew by pew, lighting candles that churchgoers had been given before the service began, for a candlelight vigil. Everyone softly sang *Silent Night* as the vigil took place. As Brianna made her way ever closer to us, my mom glanced at the church program. She read the line *Acolyte: Brianna Kurth.*

She pointed, and looked at me saying, "Brianna Kurth ... isn't that?" Her eyes were wide.

Before my mother had a chance to finish her sentence, Brianna was there at the end of the pew with a candle illuminating her beautiful face. That moment is burned in my brain as a God Sighting: a moment suspended in time, of God reaching down to Earth, making His presence known through an obvious sign of His Love.

It was the most surreal experience of my life, being presented with this gift on Christmas Eve. All my life I had dreamed of meeting my biological families, and all my life I thought of it as some far off dream to be pursued one day when I had my ducks in a row. On Christmas Eve of 2010, I didn't have ducks. I didn't have a row. I had squirrels and they were at a rave. My life was a mess, but God decided in His perfect timing to give me the ultimate Christmas gift.

Everything after the candlelight vigil is a blur in my mind. Before I knew it, the service had ended, the lights went back up, and I was staring blankly at my mother, in a daze.

"What should I do?" I asked.

Not missing a beat, she said, "Well, let's go say hi!" a huge grin spreading across her face. Her reaction exemplifies the abundant positivity and joy that she radiates to the world.

"Okay, let's go change my life forever," I said with a laugh, trying to shrug off the enormity of the moment.

I walked over to where Brianna was standing in the back of the church, having just finished her acolyte duties. I didn't know exactly how to proceed. *Hi, I'm your long-lost sister, nice to meet you?* I decided to take a simpler approach.

"Hi," I said, smiling. "Do you know who I am?"

"Yes." Brianna responded. "Let's go find Dad."

Dad? Wow. I was amazed at her simple acceptance that I was, indeed, her long-lost sister. She grabbed me gently by the arm and started leading me over to where her (*our?!*) family had been sitting. Brianna and I are nearly carbon copies of each other. I can only imagine Todd's emotions when he saw the both of us walking toward him, side by side.

I walked up and simply said, "Hi," tears forming in my eyes.

"Hi," he responded. And after a brief pause, "Oh my god, Hi!" clasping a hand to his mouth, overcome by emotion.

"This is the best Christmas ever," Todd said to me, his voice breaking.

"It is for me too," I said.

Even though I had no personal contact with this person for my entire life, except for a few letters, we hugged and I felt the strange sensation that I somehow knew and loved him in another lifetime. The years seemed to melt away in an instant. The tears were flowing all around by then. Everyone was completely overcome with joy and amazement by what had just transpired.

Todd's wife, Jamie, and my mom had the sense to snap photos and exchange contact information. Jamie and Todd insisted that anytime I wanted to call or come and visit, they'd love to have me. My sisters were excited to have finally met their big sister, whom they had only heard about through letters and pictures. It was a major shift in everything I knew as normal, but from that day forward, the Kurth Family became a permanent part of my life.

I was thirty years old before I realized that my sisters had felt the same way before meeting me ... that there was somehow a void in their hearts that needed to be filled. All those years, I simply thought that they had filled a place in my life, but I was overjoyed to realize that the feeling was mutual. I had worried that on some level they would be resentful or jealous of me coming back into my birth father's life, taking some of his attention away from them. Even if that was the case at any point, it certainly isn't now, and Brianna is the one who made that obvious to me.

When I was thirty, Brianna was a freshman in college. She was taking her general courses and had to write an essay, with the topic being an experience that changed her life. I was honored that she chose to write about our Christmas Eve of 2010.

My Christmas Miracle: By Brianna Kurth

I always knew I had an older half-sister growing up. We looked so much alike that when I was little and my parents would show me pictures of her and ask me who she was, I would say, "That's me!" In middle school, I would brag to my friends that my sister was a model and show off her pictures to my classmates. I dreamed of meeting her one day. Little did I know, one day, fate would make us cross paths and my life would be forever changed.

Ten years ago, on Christmas Eve, my family and I packed into the back of the Chevy and headed to church on that cold and snowy night. I was acolyting for the first time, and I was nervous to say the least. Once we arrived, I ran into the small church to the back room to throw on my robe before the service began because, as usual, I was late. The service started, I lit the candles that needed lighting, and my job was basically done until the end of church. At one point in the service, I noticed my mom trying to catch my attention. My parents were in the front row, and I was standing behind the pastor as she was delivering the sermon. My mom was trying to use her fingers to spell something in the air, and I knew it started with an 'L' and 'O' but I couldn't catch the rest. I thought she was trying to tell me that my shirt was too low, so I kept pulling it up. I was feeling embarrassed as I was almost directly behind the pastor so I knew she could see my mother acting crazy in the front pew. Only later did I find out that she was attempting to spell my sister's name, Lori.

My parents had been handing out programs as people walked into church that night, and saw that my sister had walked in with her parents. Throughout the whole service, they were attempting to tell me what I never could have expected, that the piece of the family that had always felt like it was missing was there with us that very night.

The final song in the service was *Silent Night*, and it was my job to pass out candles to the congregation. This is when my mom finally got the chance to tell me what was going on.

She eagerly whispered, "Lori is here!"

At first, I honestly didn't put it together that the Lori she was talking about was my sister.

I asked, "Who!?"

My dad excitedly replied, "Your sister! She is in the back pew."

I felt my face get hot. I could hear my heart beating powerfully in my ears. I don't remember handing out candles to the next few rows, but I do remember approaching the back row. She was sitting on the end, and as I handed her a candle I was staring at her and thought, *This is it, this is my chance.*

But the only words I could quietly muster were, "Here you go."

She kindly replied, "Thank you!" and smiled.

As I walked away, I was thinking that I blew my chance, I should have said something more. I couldn't wait for the service to be over.

Suddenly my mind took me to a year prior, sitting in a downtown café with my dad. We were composing a message to my sister over Facebook about how I always knew about her and that one day I would like to meet her. She responded that although she wanted to, she didn't feel that she was ready yet to meet a whole new family.

The fear of rejection washed over me. *What if she still wasn't ready? What if she never wants to meet me, that she's content with her life and her family the way it is?*

The rest of the service felt like it took an eternity. As I stood anxiously in the back collecting the candles, I kept going over what I would say if I got another chance.

My sister's family and mine were some of the last people in the church. My heart was racing as I noticed my sister start to walk toward me. We locked eyes and she smiled! I was frozen, not knowing what to do or what, if anything, to say.

She came up to me and calmly said, "Hi, I think I'm your sister."

I can't remember what I said back because I think I blacked out. We embraced and my eyes started to well up with tears, we cried and we laughed. She asked where the rest of the family was. I took her over to my parents and my younger sister. We were all in happy tears and hugging.

As my dad hugged my sister, he wept, "This is the best Christmas present ever!"

And I couldn't agree more. I stood back during the commotion and took it all in. There was a sense of peace that washed over me as I felt like my family was finally complete.

Flash-forward to present day and I can't imagine what my life would be like if fate hadn't brought us all together on that special Christmas Eve night. My sister and I became very close and we talk almost every day. She has become such an important person in my life and got me through some difficult times. I now have the cutest seven-month-old nephew whom I absolutely adore. I still think to myself all the time how lucky I am that both of our families went to the same church that night, and if it wasn't

for a Christmas Eve miracle I would not have gotten the chance
to meet my big sister."

Eight years after our Christmas Eve miracle, I sat in a pew at Saint Ignatius
Catholic Church in Houghton, Michigan. Houghton is a tiny town in Michigan's upper peninsula where the snowfall averages three hundred inches
per year. Its inhabitants are mainly families that have been there for generations, originally settling in the area for the mining all along the copper-rich
Keweenaw Peninsula. It is also a college town. Michigan Tech is ranked as
one of the top 100 engineering schools in the U.S. This combination of the
old and the new gives Houghton its charming and welcoming atmosphere.

Christmas Eve of 2018 found me in a much different place than I had
been in 2010. I was calm, joyful, and married to the love of my life, expecting our first child. I was surrounded by the glow of my loving family, and all
seemed right with the world.

Halfway through the Christmas mass, the priest took his post at the
lectern to deliver his sermon. Christmas 2018 marked the two-hundredth
anniversary of the song, *Silent Night*. As the priest rattled off some of the
history behind the famous hymn, I reminisced about that *Silent Night* candlelight vigil in 2010 and the profound impact it has had on my life and so many
others. It wasn't just my life that was better because I came to know my birth
family. A sense of loss had been felt for years by my birth father as well, and
our Christmas Eve meeting had closed that chasm. Not only that, but I was
blessed to know that my sisters felt a sense of completeness after we were
reunited as well.

As I listened to the priest's sermon, he spoke to my heart. *Silent Night*
originated at a time when a little church in Austria had fallen on financial
hardship. Their pipe organ had broken down, and since the congregation
was small and without many financial resources, there would be no funds
to fix it before Christmas Eve. Not wanting a Christmas to go by without the
joyful hymns the congregation loved to sing, the priest at the little Austrian
parish got to work. He had written *Silent Night* as a poem the previous year,
and a member of his congregation put it to music and played it on the guitar

for their Christmas Eve church service. Obviously, the song became a major hit, as we have been singing it at Christmas time in churches around the world ever since.

The priest at that little church in Houghton, Michigan, went on to say that if there hadn't been any hard times at that little church in Austria, that beloved hymn might never have come into existence. The same can be said for so many situations in our lives. The hard times put the shine into the diamond. The turbulent time of the abusive relationship I was stuck in when that Christmas Eve of 2010 came around helped me to appreciate the blessing of a new family to love, even more so than if everything had been perfect in my life at the time.

We can even say the same for the Christmas story itself. Jesus came into the world at a time of darkness under the rule of Caesar. Jews were being persecuted and many families feared for their lives and safety. In the midst of the chaos that surrounded those ancient times, a tiny baby was born in the lowliest of places, a manger. Whether or not you are a Christian, we all know that Jesus's life and work changed the course of history. Christians believe that the Christmas story sets the tone for our lives. God's selfless act of love in sending his only son to Earth to live, and later die for us, is the ultimate example of unconditional love. At Christmas time, we strive to emulate this by expressing our love to those around us: family and friends, strangers, even people we may not like very much.

So, it is at Christmas time that I always reflect on the amazing gifts that I've been given. Not the material kind, but the gifts of love, family, and faith.

Christmas was such an appropriate time for the gift of reconnection with my birth family. Now that I have children of my own, I can begin to try to understand the tremendous sacrifice that Todd and Adrienne made in placing me for adoption. As God bestowed Jesus on the world, sacrificing his only son, Adrienne and Todd gave me a chance for a better life, and they gave my parents the gift of becoming a family of three. Sacrifice is the most selfless form of love.

CHAPTER 6:

❦

The Kurth Clan, 2011–2014

AFTER THAT CHRISTMAS EVE IN 2010, I entered into a new era of self-dis-covery in my life. I left my abusive relationship with Carter and I was finally figuring out who I was as an individual. Todd and his family played a huge role in helping me do this.

The summer of 2011 was a time of bonding and breakthroughs for all of us. I started spending as much time as I could in Minocqua with Todd and his family. It was the first time in my adult life that I had the opportunity to explore my identity without the hindrance of a boyfriend and, more impor-tantly, without the abuse of one. My first summer with the Kurths healed a lot of hurts for me. The time I spent with them felt like walking into the arms of unconditional love itself. The relationships I began to build with them filled a void that had been inside me for my whole life. For the first time, I didn't feel like I needed a significant other to validate my own identity, and I know my newfound relationship with my biological family had a lot to do with that. I began discovering new and deeper facets of who I am.

July 4, 2011 was the first time I met some of the extended Kurth family. Todd and Jamie invited me to their big shindig, which took place in Minocqua, Wisconsin. I have social anxiety, so the prospect of meeting a multitude of new people all at once literally made me nauseated. I knew that once again my life was about to irreversibly change. I knew it would be for the better, but it was nerve-wracking nonetheless. It's such a strange feeling knowing that you're about to meet relatives whom you have never met, or at least you don't remember meeting, knowing that they already care about you and want to be a part of your life.

I drove Up North to meet them all and my mind raced thinking of all the possible ways the day might unfold. Let me take you on a tangent here to explain the phrase, "Up North." To Midwesterners, Up North is a special place. It's more than just a place that is north of where you usually live. It's a peaceful place filled with campfires, starry nights, lakes and rivers, and relaxation. Up North is different for everyone, but it's more of a feeling than a place. The Minocqua area, where the Kurths lived, has always been my Up North.

The Fourth of July event of 2011 was taking place on Lake Minocqua at a local hangout, Torpy Park. Lake Minocqua is the central lake in a chain of three lakes that everyone cruises around on in the summer. Torpy Park is prime real estate because it's right in the middle of the chain, it has a swimming beach and boat landing, and it boasts lots of areas for picnics and barbecuing in the green grass. The coveted tables and picnic spots at the park were all but completely taken over when I arrived on that Fourth of July. Little did I know as I approached Todd that it was mainly the Kurth family who had claimed them all! Barbecuing, boating, and beer were abundant that day. It can never be said that the Kurth clan doesn't know how to have a good time!

As I walked across the park to meet Todd, I thought, *What business do I have inserting myself into this entire family when I barely even know Todd yet?*

The whole situation felt absurd. It seemed like every person there had locked their gaze on me as I approached. However, my feelings of uneasiness were short lived as I was quickly introduced to at least a dozen people and I was swept up in hugs and raucous laughter.

Attending the Fourth of July event turned out to be one of the best decisions I ever could have made. Because of that day, I met aunts, uncles, cousins, grandparents, and many others who welcomed me into Todd's family with open arms. We spent the day eating, drinking, tubing, swimming, and just enjoying each other's company.

Once it was dark outside, we watched the fireworks from the comfort of Todd's Centurion boat in the middle of Lake Minocqua. We had the best seat in the house! Minocqua's Fourth of July fireworks are the place to be, and people line up their lawn chairs for blocks along the lake to get a good seat. Being out on the water is like having a front-row VIP ticket. After the fireworks were over, we spent some time waiting for the boat traffic to thin out. My then nine-year-old sister Morgan and I had a dance off on the back of the boat deck to Katy Perry's *California Girls*, which was the hit single of the summer. Everyone was in stitches watching us dance together. Even passersby on other boats were cheering us on. I simply couldn't believe that after years of not knowing any of these people, I was magically a part of the family. It all seemed too good to be true.

One of our classic family jokes originated that night. After a fun-filled day with family, we kept the party going. My close friend Amanda was in Minocqua for the holiday, and she met up with us later in the day. We went out to the local bars with Todd, Todd's brother Clint, and Clint's wife, Leah. We took Todd's boat through the chain of lakes and hit up a few different places. Bars and restaurants turn their biggest profits of the year when tourists come for the summer and take advantage of barhopping by boat. One of the most popular spots on the water is called The Thirsty Whale. This is where we finished our evening of fun.

Todd, Clint, and I were out on the deck drinking beer from Clint's beer horn, a homemade beer bong, and Amanda was inside talking to some random dude. If you knew Amanda and I in our early twenties, a scene such as this one was typical. After cheering on Clint's chug from the beer horn, I heard a song that I loved playing inside the bar, so I made a mad dash for the dance floor. Little did I know that the floor of the bar was soaking wet from spilled beer and boaters traipsing in and out of the establishment all day. The second I stepped inside, I completely wiped out, flat on the floor in full view of everyone. From that point on, The Thirsty Whale became known as The Slippery Whale in the Kurth family. It is an inside joke that we laugh about to this day.

As time wore on, I became deeply connected with Todd, Jamie, and my sisters. As I have already stated, they helped piece together parts of my past and present that I had previously been trying to gloss over and fill in by wasting my time with shitty boyfriends. I could tell Todd and Jamie things I couldn't tell my own parents because our relationship felt more like a friendship than a parent-to-child relationship. In those late summer nights of 2011, I often talked to Todd about my struggles, hopes, dreams, and joys. Jamie was an angel, letting me step into her family as if I had always been there, supporting me every step of the way.

In 2015, I was introduced to even more of my biological family through a family reunion. Todd's parents divorced when he was a child, but he remained close with his biological father. Todd's last name, Kurth, is actually the name of his stepfather, who legally adopted him. A man by the name of Wayne Schultz is Todd's biological father. The Schultz family is one of the most tenderhearted, compassionate, funny, and welcoming groups of people you could ever hope to meet.

In 2015, the Schultz Family Reunion was held in San Diego, California. Todd, Jamie, Morgan, Brianna, Jamie's mom, Karen, and I all boarded a plane to Los Angeles to attend! From the moment we arrived at the airport, the entire trip was nothing but nonstop laughs.

Jamie's mom, Karen, doesn't travel much. She definitely was not up to snuff on some of the tighter security restrictions and what you can or cannot say in an airport. She brought hard-boiled eggs as a snack for the time we would spend on the plane (*Everybody does that, right?*) and we had been giving her grief about it. Before we even got to the airport, we told her they might be confiscated by security. Karen said, "Oh, for Pete's sake, what are they gonna think? That they're grenades or something?"

We went through TSA screening and they weren't taken away. At the end of the security line Karen said, at a normal and somewhat loud volume, "Well, the egg grenades made it through!" We were all so shocked we didn't even say anything. We were just thankful that she didn't get arrested right then and there!

When we arrived in Los Angeles, we rented a car and decided to tour the city and see a few sights before driving to San Diego. We immediately went to see the famous Hollywood sign. On our way up into the Hollywood Hills, we pulled into a golf course to potentially grab a bite to eat at the club-house restaurant. A golfer accidentally dropped his GoPro camera right in front of our minivan immediately when we drove past looking for a park-ing spot.

Crunch.

"Oh!" Jamie, who was driving, said. "What was that?"

"Drive," Todd said. "Well girls, we ain't eatin' here today! I'm not paying for a new GoPro camera for butterfingers back there!" Some poor schmuck in California probably still tells the story of how his brand new GoPro was crushed by a minivan full of tourists.

I came to learn that the Schultz family shared a multitude of my person-ality traits, It was fascinating to me when I began to realize that there are parts of my personality that are simply genetic. My slightly off-color sense of humor, sometimes-rebellious nature, and penchant for partying are all Todd traits, along with my huge heart and empathy toward others. I have always had FOMO (fear of missing out), and that's a Todd trait as well. That's why, to this day, we will stay up all night every time we see each other, having beers and catching up. We don't want to miss a minute. Todd not only accepted, he understood my personality quirks. This gave me the confidence and space to begin to grow into the person I wanted to be: Myself. I had finally started to feel comfortable in my own skin.

CHAPTER 7:

<del></del>

A Difficult Year

THE YEAR 2011 CAME AND went in the blink of an eye. My final year of college began in 2012. It was the year from hell.

As I have touched on previously, I am very close with my mom who raised me. By my senior year of college, I was more of a responsible adult than a child she had to look out for and our relationship shifted. We became best friends. The advice I once scoffed at as a teen became sought after and valued. We talked on the phone almost daily and laughed about the ups and downs in life.

At the point when our new relationship as friends was at its finest, my mother was diagnosed for the second time in two years with breast cancer. It was a shocking blow.

I remember the phone call well. I was walking to my Dance for Camera class and it was a beautiful spring day. I was excitedly considering different themes for the dance piece I wanted to create. Dance for Camera was a class reserved specifically for seniors, and it involved creating a dance production for film. At the end of the semester, there was a special screening of the dance pieces in one of the theaters in the Noel Fine Arts Building. Since my freshman year, I had been excited to produce my dance film. I was playing with the idea of incorporating candlelight and telling a portion of my Christmas Eve story, highlighting my relationship with my newfound birth family.

Per usual, I had called my mom to catch up as I walked to campus. I was bursting with creative energy and I wanted to bounce my ideas off of her before presenting them in class that day. Professor Karen had warned us that she'd be choosing us at random to discuss our themes beginning that day in class, so I really wanted to be prepared.

My mom listened intently to me, but something in her tone was off as we spoke. I remember that I was walking into the courtyard of the communications building and the crabapple trees were flowering when she laid her cards on the table.

"Honey, I have to tell you something."

I stopped dead in my tracks. I clearly remember telling myself at that moment in time that nothing bad could possibly happen on such a beautiful day, surrounded by flowering spring loveliness.

"I found another lump."

Those four words hit me like a ton of bricks, especially because my mother had undergone a bilateral mastectomy in 2010, in order to prevent the cancer from ever returning. I was rendered speechless. She went on, "I'm having a biopsy done at the end of the week."

I swallowed the lump in my throat and said, "I love you, Mom. Everything is going to be okay."

I went into class in a daze, completely shell-shocked by what I had just heard. I was praying I wouldn't be one of the first picked to meet with Professor Karen to present my ideas. Of course, I was. She sensed my vulnerability and preyed on it, because that's the type of person she is.

She said, with a wild look in her eye, "Something's different today, no?" She shrugged exaggeratedly, like a mime putting on a performance.

I shared with her the serious nature of the phone call I had received just before class. Any normal person would react with sympathy and concern, but she laughed her maniacal pixie laugh and spewed some garbage about pressing on in a fake French accent. I am not even joking. She honestly decided who she wanted to be on a daily basis and took on those characteristics whole-heartedly. Apparently, that day she was a jovial French artiste without a care in the world.

When we found out that the biopsy was positive for cancer, we couldn't believe the disease had come back despite the extreme preventive measures my mother had taken. Initially, things seemed bleak. My mom was scared, and so was I. I was a wreck while she underwent treatments. The possibility that I could lose my mother, who had become my best friend, seemed all too real. Thankfully, after radiation, the cancer went into remission. She has now been cancer-free for nearly ten years.

In the course of that tumultuous time, an old flame made his way back onto my radar. Trent and I dated during my senior year of high school and most of my freshman year of college. We had ended on bad terms—I dumped him to date Carter, and clearly that did not work out well for me—and I had not heard from him since 2009. I was surprised when I saw a message pop up in my Facebook inbox from him.

Having heard about my mother's health, he reached out to express his sympathies and support.

Hey, Lori. I heard about what your mom is going through. She is honestly the nicest person I have ever met. I am sorry she has to deal with this. I am thinking of your family.

I stared blankly at the screen after reading the message. My initial reaction was, *WTF?* followed by some laughter at the absurdity of his timing. I decided to send a message back thanking him for reaching out. We kept the discussion going for a while that evening, and he brought it to my attention that he would be passing through Stevens Point the next day. He offered to take me out to dinner. I recklessly accepted even though I knew that Trent and I had never been anything but bad for each other.

What harm can one dinner possibly do? I thought to myself. I needed someone in my life who was separate from the chaos, a distraction. That night marked the beginning of our slow descent back into a relationship. I didn't want to open up to anyone close to me because that would make my situation too real. I was trying to be strong for my mom, and I didn't want to admit how out of control and scared I felt. After that first dinner, I began talking to Trent almost daily. He was funny and entertaining. He was a great listener and didn't really say much when I just needed to vent. He understood me in ways that other people didn't because he knew who I was before adulthood began to change me. He took me out every time he was in town and, sooner rather than later, he began making special trips to see me weekly. He courted me the old-fashioned way all summer, and by fall of 2012 we were officially back together.

In November of 2012, my mother was a month out from her last cancer treatment. She was healing well and in good spirits. Everything seemed to be settling down, and we were all relieved that she was nearly back to perfect health. My relationship with Trent was going strong, and he and I were finishing up our senior year of college, spending our free time together whenever we could. I was preparing for graduation with happy anticipation for what the future might hold, and he was preparing to take his LSAT and then apply to University of Wisconsin–Madison for law school.

I went home to visit my parents for the weekend often, and decided to make the trip one afternoon in late November after clocking some hours for the Susan G. Komen internship I was working at that semester. Naturally, when the opportunity arose to work in health education, specifically related to women's health and breast cancer, I jumped at it. I interviewed, got the position on the spot, and I loved every minute of it. In a way, I felt like I was doing my small part to help other women so that they would never have to endure what my mom went through, or feel the pain of watching someone they love suffer through cancer.

On that beautiful fall Friday, I walked through the front door of my childhood home and I was delighted when I discovered that my mom's best friend, Sally, had also stopped by. Sally and my mom had been friends for decades, and she was like a second mom to me. When I walked into the kitchen, she and my mom were deep into dreaming up and plotting out their next trip. For years, Sally had been traveling with my mom and I. Every trip we took together was always exponentially more fun because Sal was there. She could even turn a trip to the gas station into a memorable adventure!! We traveled to the Bahamas, Florida, New York City, and as far as Australia together. Sally often came on day trips to dinner theaters or the Mall of America with us. Her laughter was contagious and she and my mom were like the real-life version of Lucille Ball and Ethel Mertz.

When I walked into the kitchen, I saw the two of them crowded around the computer, looking up everything they could about the U.K., Scotland, and Ireland. Sally was an adventurer like my mom, and it was her dream to visit these places. I had to laugh when I observed the scene, both of them so intent on what they were up to that they hadn't even heard me come in the front door. At the sound of my laughter, they both turned around to see me.

"Well, Hi, Lori!!!" Sally said. When she said something as simple as hello, she had a way of completely warming your soul. "We're up to no good!" she said, and broke out in a peal of her contagious laughter.

"What is it now?" I asked with a grin.

"Well, we're just planning our next adventure! And hey, if you can get the time off from school, we'd love for you to come with us!" my mom said.

The three of us sat around laughing and talking for hours. That's just how it always was with Sal. She genuinely cared about everyone and always wanted to know all the details of your life. Hours passed like seconds whenever she was around.

The following weekend, I went home again for a visit. I walked into the house to find my mom on the phone with Sally. When I found out it was her, I asked to say hi before they hung up. Sal and I talked for about fifteen minutes and she asked about college, dance, who I was seeing, everything. I told her about my job at a dance studio in Stevens Point and invited her to come the following weekend to take one of my Zumba classes.

"It's so much fun, Sal. Anyone can do it. Mom is going and I'm sure she'd love the company if you came and took the class with her!"

Sally chuckled. "Are you sure I could handle it? I'm so out of shape, Lori!"

"Sal, don't worry! Zumba is just a big, fun dance party. It's low pressure. And besides, if my mom can do it, you can too!"

Sally laughed. "Okay, you convinced me! I'll be there with bells on!"

Later in the week, Sally called my mom to change up her plans. She had forgotten about a trip that she and her husband were taking that weekend with another couple. She begged off the Zumba class and asked my mom if she'd mind taking Scout, her yellow lab, for the weekend. Of course, my mom was happy to help out. I was a little disappointed when my mom told me that Sally couldn't come to the class anymore, but I understood.

Thursday night, Sally dropped Scout off at my parents' house, as she and her husband were leaving on the train to Chicago bright and early the next morning. That evening, I called my mom to confirm the time of the Zumba class on Saturday and make sure she was still coming. I could hear Scout and my family dog, Sadie, roughhousing in the background. It made me laugh. Scout and Sadie were best buds, just like my mom and Sal.

On Friday night, Trent and I went out to dinner in Stevens Point. He was scheduled to take his LSAT the next day and he had been studying like a madman for months. It was his dream to attend UW–Madison's School of Law, and his score on the LSAT would determine whether or not he would make the cut for admission. My cell phone rang during our meal, and seeing that it was my mother, I ignored it. I figured she was calling to double-check some details about the Zumba class the next day. *I'll call her after dinner*, I thought, and let the call go to voicemail.

Trent and I had finished dinner and he had just pulled into the parking lot of my dorm when I listened to the voicemail. The news I heard came as a total shock.

My mother's voice came through shaky and she had obviously been crying.

"Hi honey, it's Mom. I'm calling to let you know that my very best friend Sally died today of a massive heart attack."

Her words were strained and she could barely get them out. It simply couldn't be true. I had just talked to Sally a week ago. She was in Chicago on vacation! There was no way she had met the fate my mother described. I replayed the voicemail to make sure I had heard it correctly. The second time I heard it, it began to sink in. I felt like I had been run over by a freight train. Sally wouldn't be at Zumba the next day because Sally was dead. The phone conversation we'd had just a week before was our last. My whole body convulsed with sobs as I began to realize the full impact of what had happened. My phone fell out of my hand into the center console.

Trent had been watching all of this unfold from the driver's seat of the car and was extremely concerned by this point.

"What? What is it Lori? Lori, what?" he asked.

I couldn't speak or move. He just kept repeating himself. "What happened? Is it your mom?"

He knew I worried about my mom's health every single day since her battle with cancer. He knew that my biggest fear in the world was losing her. I managed to shake my head. Finally, I handed him my phone and told him to listen to the voicemail. I couldn't bear to speak the words I'd just heard.

"Oh, wow. Oh, my god," he said as he heard it. "I'm so sorry, baby." He held me as I cried for what seemed like an eternity inside his little Mazda. So much for his relaxing night before the LSAT. He finally suggested that we go in and try to get some sleep. I was so worn out from crying that I slept like a rock that night.

I slept so deeply that I was up and fully awake by six am the following morning. I had spoken to my mother the night before and she was still planning to come to the Zumba class I had to teach at ten a.m. Her strength is incredible. Losing her best friend, and still willing to spend an hour round trip in the car to drive to and participate in an upbeat workout class the very next day.

I took a walk outside to try to clear my head a little. I stood outside my dorm on that first day of December, trying to get my head around what had happened and how I would manage to teach as if nothing were going on, especially with my mom as a class participant. All I really wanted to do was hold my mother tight and cry and cry with her.

I had parked myself on top of a picnic table as I took in the fresh air, trying to clear my mind. Suddenly, my cell phone rang. It was Todd calling. He must have seen the Facebook post I'd made regarding Sally's death.

"Hi, Sunshine. How ya doing?" he asked in a caring tone.

Just the simple question sent me into a tailspin. I got choked up and couldn't speak.

"Sorry, that was a stupid question," he said. "I know you're feeling like shit right now."

His blunt matter-of-factness made me laugh through my tears. We spoke for a few minutes and then Jamie got on the phone with me as well. She and Todd expressed words of love and support, holding me up like the lifesaver I needed to get through that day. Usually my mother was the pillar of strength in my life, but just like when she went through cancer treatments, this was a time where I had to be strong for her, and not the other way around. It meant the world to me that Todd and Jamie had reached out to me that day to let me know they were there for me. I hung up the phone and found a way to pull myself together. I taught the Zumba class. My mom fully participated. And then she went back home to help Sally's husband get some of her affairs in order, like the heart-of-gold badass that she is.

A few days later, I received a care package from Jamie in the mail. In it, she had included the book *Heaven is for Real* by Todd Burpo. The book was written by a pastor whose son went through a life-threatening illness and emergency surgery. Months after the ordeal, the little boy began recounting details of his experience and how he had gone to Heaven and back and claimed to have had the chance to meet Jesus. Jamie wrote a note to me and attached it with the book.

Lori-

*I read this book when my Grandma passed and I was having a
very hard time. I hope you find the same comfort in it that I did.
We love you!*

I fully believe in a deeper connection between children and God, and the
spiritual realm. This account of a child's experience of visiting Heaven and
returning to earth resonated deeply in my soul and comforted me. I have
always loved working with children for their total honesty and innocence.
It was these qualities that made the book *Heaven is for Real* so readable and
convincing. From that point forward, I clung to my faith like a life preserver
in the middle of a stormy sea. I had to believe in God and I had to believe in
Heaven or I simply could not accept reality as it was. Unfortunately, I clung
to my relationship with Trent in exactly the same manner.

Trent came back to me in between the beginning of my mother's cancer
treatments and the sudden death of one of the most important people in my
life. In hindsight, I know it was wrong to jump back into a relationship with
him. I loved him in a platonic way, like you love a best friend or a comfortable
old pair of jeans. He loved me much more fiercely than that. It really wasn't
fair of me to take advantage of his feelings. If I was the sun in his universe,
he was only a star in mine. I clung to him because he was something famil-
iar and reliable in a tumultuous time. This only escalated the intensity of our
relationship, and by the beginning of 2013, we were engaged.

Todd never liked Trent very much. Honestly, no one in my life did. He
was smart but not social, attractive but not amiable. Todd was the only one
who was bold enough to say something to me about it. It infuriated me at the
time, but it also made me take stock of things. I could see that my fiancé was
not someone who got along with many people. It depressed me to think that
he would never share in the kind of family closeness and laughter that the
Kurth family exemplified. It saddened me that I'd never be able to introduce
my husband to my friends and family without carrying the conversation for
him. I began to wonder if he was the kind of person with whom I could raise

a family, rather than just someone who could provide financially but would never be there for our kids or me emotionally.

Trent's dreams came true and he was accepted into the law school at UW–Madison. When he moved to Madison for school in the fall of 2013, our relationship took a turn for the worse. It died a slow, tortured death caused by distance and a lack of commitment on his end. Over the months, I realized that I was always his last priority. Law school, his overbearing and manipulative mother, and his friends mattered most to him, in that exact order. His mother may have actually trumped law school when I stop to think about it. So, while I wore myself thin working two jobs and driving to Madison every weekend to see him, he constantly put me on the back burner. Many small offenses slowly turned into an insurmountable pile of bullshit by the spring of 2014. One day, I was just done. It took every ounce of strength in my soul, but I called off the engagement and left him. My wedding dress was purchased. My save the dates had been ordered. I'd booked a DJ and a reception venue. But none of it mattered when I took into account how miserable I knew I would be for the rest of my life with someone who didn't respect me or care about my values. I made him a priority, while to him I was an option.

I still vividly remember the time I spent talking with Todd when I was back and forth about the situation. I had spent most of the afternoon in tears and he talked me down from my indecisiveness and fear with common sense. He was part of my strength in walking away from a relationship that would have destroyed my life. In more ways than one, my reunion with my biological family saved me.

CHAPTER 8:

⋙

Yo, Adrienne!

It was during this chaotic time of ups and downs with my former fiancé that I reached out to my birth mother, Adrienne. I had dreamed of meeting her for my entire life. I had spent three years getting to know Todd and his family, and I felt that the time had come to take the next step. I wrote Adrienne a letter in August of 2013 and then sat on it for months. I was mostly ready to meet her, but a part of me was scared. In the same way that meeting my birth father and his huge family had rocked my world, I knew that meeting Adrienne would do the same. I was also worried that the opposite of what I wanted would happen. What if she had heard through the grapevine that I reconnected with Todd's family and not with her? What if she thought it was deliberate, and she felt slighted and wanted nothing to do with me? Could I handle it if that was what happened?

I had always known that Todd and his family wanted to meet me when the time was right, because of their letters and from Brianna reaching out to me. However, I didn't know if Adrienne would be ready or willing to meet me, and whether or not her family would be accepting of me if I did develop a relationship with her. I was beyond anxious at the thought of turning my life upside down again, yet the still, small voice in my heart told me that I had to do it.

I finally sent the letter to Adrienne in January of 2014. I should add that this was in large part due to Todd's wife, Jamie. Jamie knew that I had wanted to reconnect with Adrienne and that I had been hanging on to that letter for months. There was a period of time when every visit to the Kurths meant that Jamie would ask me, "Did you send it?" What a blessing that my birth father's wife was so supportive of my reunion with my birth mother! If it weren't for her, I would have waited even longer than I did!

I received a letter back from Adrienne a few weeks later, saying that she wanted to meet me, too. She included her contact information and we agreed that I would meet her at her home in Wisconsin Rapids in early February of 2014. We never spoke on the phone, instead we texted each other to set up the date. We both felt that something as major as hearing each other's voices for the first time should happen in person.

The night before my meeting with Adrienne, I sat up writing in my diary:

> Well, here it goes again. My life is about to change forever tomorrow. The day I've always dreamed of is nearly here!

The hour-long drive to reach Adrienne's home was laden with pure adrenaline. I thought about turning around and going home. I thought about just continuing to drive … spontaneous road trip, destination unknown! Every mile passed slowly, yet lightning fast at the same time. I knew that the end of my journey would fulfill a lifelong dream, but I had no idea how the next chapters of my story would unfold once it was realized. The not knowing was driving me the craziest of all.

I pulled up in her circular drive, taking in her beautiful home. I sat in the car for a moment, contemplating just staying there until someone came out to get me or just turning around and pretending like I hadn't initiated the situation at all. Part of me wanted to march up to the front door and make my dreams come true, and another part of me wanted to disappear. I knew at that moment that what I had always wanted was right in front of me, so I took a deep breath and got out of my car. I walked up to her front door and rang the bell. My heart was in my throat and I felt like I could just about jump right out of my skin.

I took a shaky breath and moments later, the door slowly opened. The person I saw looking back at me seemed like a reflection of my own face, but maybe fifteen years older. I felt as though I were looking into my future as I stared into my birth mother's eyes.

We immediately embraced in the doorway and the tears flowed freely. Adrienne's husband, Daryl, stood off to the side. He had been taking photos of our first moments together. I cut into the waterfall of emotions with a simple, "Hi, Daryl!"

We all laughed.

The rest of the day flew by in a blur. Neither of us knew what to expect, but we ended up spending more than five hours together on that first day, talking, and learning about each other.

Call it mother's intuition, call it a coincidence, but Adrienne knew from that first meeting that Trent wasn't the one for me. She said as much to Daryl, but not to me. I remember sitting on her couch that day and telling her about my relationship and how we had gotten engaged because it was the next logical step. After I left that evening, Adrienne sat talking with Daryl.

"I just don't think that this Trent is the one for her. Call me crazy. Call it intuition. I don't know. But what she said today ... how their engagement was logical? Love isn't logical, it's supposed to be magical." She could tell that I wasn't in for a fairytale happy ending even before I knew it myself.

Adrienne and I spent more time together gradually over the coming months. We reunited in February, and by the beginning of May I had walked away from my relationship with Trent. I would be lying if I said that Adrienne had nothing to do with it. She came into my life at a chaotic time, and she was a beacon of light that led me to find my own inner strength. She acted like a very experienced therapist to me during those tough times.

In her younger years, Adrienne was in a relationship much like mine. She was married to a man who needed to get his priorities in order and just needed to grow up in general. When I was going through hell with Trent, we talked on the phone almost daily and she was the ever-present font of wisdom and shoulder to cry on as I fought through the agony of ending my engagement. Not once did she ever tell me what to do. She simply shared her experiences and pearls of wisdom. She was completely transparent. At one point she said to me, "If I had it to do all over again, I would have done things differently. I am so grateful for all that it taught me and for my wonderful boys. There were definitely good things that came from the relationship. For that reason, I am glad for our marriage. My life wouldn't be the same without Marty and Ben. But when I married him, I was in a difficult place and he gave me what I was lacking … a family and some stability in my life. Honey, I'd rather see you end something now than have to go through the pain and burden of a divorce like I did. If you don't see things getting any better, it's best to spare yourself and rip off the bandage now. And I don't say this to be cruel or to tell you what to do. I just see you going down a similar path and I don't want you to have to go through the hell that I went through."

When Adrienne met Mitch, her first husband, she had been through a hell of a lot in a very short period. First, she had gone through the experience of giving birth to me and putting me up for adoption. Then, in less than a year, both of her brothers passed away suddenly from a rare heart condition. Much like Adrienne, I had searched for comfort in a relationship when my own world was upside down, and much like Mitch, Trent was not ready to grow up. Adrienne was an amazing support for me as I fought my way out of a difficult time and moved into my new life, my new self. I knew I had to walk away, and she was there for me when I took the first step.

CHAPTER 9:

SBA

As I GOT TO KNOW my birth mother, we were both amused by how alike we are. Even though I didn't know her until my mid-twenties, we quickly discovered that we have a multitude of personality and physical traits in common. We give nature versus nurture a run for its money. One of our most obvious shared traits is our sense of humor.

One example of our similar sense of humor occurred on a cold winter night in 2015. Adrienne, Daryl, my boyfriend (now husband) Sean, and I were all out to dinner in Wisconsin Rapids. As was our precedent and as is customary in small Northern Wisconsin towns, many a cocktail or beer was enjoyed before, during, and after dinner. We had finished our meals and were hanging out at the restaurant's main bar when the owner, John, came out to say hello. He hadn't met me yet and wanted to see the mysterious daughter Adrienne had reunited with, and say hello to his old friends.

Let me pause for a moment to tell you that the moment someone first sees me with Adrienne never gets old. Their facial expressions say it all. Often they do a double take and are left speechless. I look startlingly like my birth mother, sixteen years younger. When I first met Adrienne, I felt like I was looking into a mirror that showed me my future … and, thankfully, we have some great genes in our family! Most people seem to see the same thing I did. Adrienne has a little grandson named Layton. The first time I met Layton he was four years old. After meeting me, Adrienne was putting him to bed that night. Before he drifted off to sleep he said, "Grandma, when I first met Lori, I thought she was you!"

John's reaction did not disappoint either. He sauntered over to us to say hello and displayed the standard reaction of shock, joy, and general disbelief at seeing the two of us side by side. Then he offered to give me a tour of his establishment. So, Adrienne and I followed him downstairs to his offices and wine cellar and he explained some of the history of the place, how his wines were selected, and other details about his supper club.

"So, now you know some of my story. Can I hear yours? How did you two manage to reconnect?"

We shared our story and some of the divine intervention we have experienced along the way. John was moved to tears. Before we went back upstairs, he asked me to choose a bottle of wine from his cellar. He insisted on it, as a token of his hospitality and gratitude for my willingness to be so open with him.

We trooped back upstairs and headed into the private dining room and bar in the back. John pulled out a cigar and lit it. Adrienne pulled out her pack of American Spirit cigarettes and gave me one as well. Like Adrienne, I only smoke when I'm drinking. Minutes later, Daryl and Sean burst through the doors.

"Well, there you guys are!" Daryl said. "We were lookin' all over for you!"

"Daryl Kingery, I told you exactly where we were going when we left. John wanted to give Lori a little tour of the place," Adrienne replied. This exchange just goes to show how many cocktails were consumed that evening.

"Jeez, what are you guys doing smoking up the place? You can't do that in here!" Sean chided us. He and Daryl had apparently taken on the role of the fun police by this point in the evening.

"This is John's place and he says I can," Adrienne replied. "Besides," she added, "We don't have to listen to you. We're super badass. We can do what we want."

Anyone who knows me would tell you that this is exactly the kind of remark that would come out of my mouth after (or even before) a few drinks. The rest of the evening we referred to ourselves as the badasses. The nickname stuck. Adrienne and I have our own Super Badass club, as we call it. She's Superbadass Number One and I'm Superbadass Number Two, kind of like Dr. Seuss's Thing One and Thing Two, only cooler. Whenever we do something extra cool or out of the ordinary, we always tell each other about our super-badass deeds. When we find something while out shopping that we deem super badass (or, as we abbreviate it, SBA), we buy it for the other. If we see someone when we are out and about who is engaging in super badass behavior, a Snapchat or text of said person will be sent. The list goes on and on. We've allowed other family members and friends into our gang, but we know that we will always be the original SBA crew. Badass-themed jewelry, apparel, and household items have become popular nowadays. But back when we started our club, they were nowhere to be found. We jokingly say that we started the trend.

A few months after the Super Badass Club came into existence, Adrienne was enjoying a summer evening with her husband, Daryl. They were having drinks in their lower garage, which is more like a rec room than an actual garage. Daryl went up to the house for a few minutes to grab some snacks for them. Moments after Daryl left, Adrienne heard a loud noise outside the garage and a thud against one of the outside walls.

"Knock it off, Daryl Kingery!" she yelled, assuming it was Daryl playing a joke on her. The noise continued, and when Adrienne popped outside to investigate, she found herself within a few feet of a hungry black bear that had been rummaging in their garbage cans for a snack. She didn't panic at all, but instead thought quickly on her feet. The Fourth of July was right around the corner, and there were a few fireworks lying around the garage. Adrienne took it upon herself to light a few off and scare the bear away. Daryl heard the commotion and came running down from the house, cheese and crackers flying off of the plate he'd just put together for the two of them.

"What in the hell's goin' on down here!?"

Adrienne explained the situation with the bear. A few minutes later, I received a text saying, "I have a new process of initiation for the SBA club. Must be willing to scare off wild animals with improvised weapons. I just shot fireworks at a bear."

The recipe of my relationship with Adrienne has been one of friendship and camaraderie, sprinkled with laughter supplied by our equally twisted senses of humor. The privilege of having her in my life has been like having a big sister or a cool aunt to look up to and laugh with. At the same time, she gives the best motherly advice and real talk when I need it. She is my hero in countless ways. Her strength is unparalleled, and I will always look up to her for her determination to never let anything get in her way. She is kind and genuine and she has never let the cruel blows that life has dealt her make her bitter. The world needs more Adriennes.

CHAPTER 10:

╼╼╼

Divine Intervention

ADRIENNE'S MOTHER, JUNE, EXPERIENCED SOME horrible things in her life. June's first husband committed suicide and his family blamed her for it. Times were different then. The doctor June saw prescribed alcohol to help her cope. By the time Adrienne was in the picture, June was an alcoholic. Adrienne was very close with her brothers, Richard and Allen. All of the kids took care of each other when June struggled with her alcoholism.

When Adrienne made the decision to put me up for adoption, no one knew that both her brothers were slowly falling victim to a rare genetic heart condition. Hypertrophic Cardiomyopathy (HCM) is a condition in which part of the heart becomes thickened without an obvious cause. This results in the heart being less able to pump blood effectively. Complications include heart failure, irregular heartbeat, and sudden cardiac death. Most people with the condition have no symptoms and don't experience any complications until it's too late. When Richard and Allen passed away within a few months of each other at ages nineteen and twenty-one, the autopsies showed that they both had classic characteristics of HCM.

God had a plan for my life and for Adrienne's, and He knew what He was doing when He led her to my parents. You thought the Christmas Eve miracle was incredible? Well, buckle up for this.

Not only is my father a cardiologist, he assisted with groundbreaking research in some of the first clinical trials using beta-blockers to treat symptoms of cardiomyopathy back in the 1970s. Of course, Adrienne didn't know any of this and my parents didn't know that the disease ran in her family when I became a part of theirs. Back then, the adoption process kept the adoptive parents' professions private from the birth parents so that finances didn't become part of the equation when choosing an adoptive family.

Wausau is a small community, and my father was able to keep tabs on how Adrienne was doing through her father, Rick, who was his patient. He was devastated to hear the news when both of her brothers passed. My dad became a permanent part of Adrienne's life from then on. He saw to it that she and her family were well taken care of medically, and he was extra vigilant in looking for signs of the disease in Adrienne and her sons. He also kept a close eye on me. I had echocardiograms performed yearly at his cardiology clinic as I was growing up to ensure that I did not have the disease. Being proactive was simple, because my father made it so.

When my half-brother, Marty, was twelve years old, he began showing symptoms of the heart condition. I vividly remember my father talking to my mother about it in the kitchen one evening. In my fourteen-year-old mind, I was torn between being fascinated with my father's skill in medicine, sad for Marty and Adrienne, and jealous that my father had contact with the people I had been waiting my whole life to meet. Marty had an echocardiogram performed at a pediatric clinic. The echo did show some abnormalities, but the cardiologist chalked them up as minor and due to normal fluctuations that any teenage athlete, such as Marty, would experience during puberty. On my father's orders, Adrienne had a copy of the echo sent to him so that he could read it himself. Knowing the genetic history of Hypertrophic Cardiomyopathy (HCM) in Adrienne's bloodline, and being the meticulous physician that he is, he immediately questioned the abnormalities. He recommended further testing for Marty and it was discovered that Marty indeed had HCM. The dedication and care that my father showed to Adrienne and her family ultimately played a role in saving Marty's life. Were it not for him, Marty might not be here with us today. His symptoms could have gone unrecognized for years, and he could have met the same fate as his uncles before him.

Adrienne chose life. There is never an easy decision when it comes to the situation she was in, but were it not for her choice to brave the full term of her unplanned pregnancy, a ripple effect would have occurred. She ultimately chose to give my parents the gift of a family. Had she not done so, she never would have met my father, who played a role in saving the life of her first-born son.

I do not have HCM. In our family, it is an x-chromosome-linked recessive trait, wherein females are the gene carriers and their male offspring express the gene fifty percent of the time. We assumed that Adrienne's mother was a gene carrier, as is Adrienne. I always knew that when I had children, I would have to consider the possibility that I might be a carrier as well.

When Sean and I were dating for about a year, I expressed this concern to him. I told him that if we were to get married and start a family one day, there was a very real possibility that I could be a carrier of the gene. I shared this with him because I couldn't in good conscience keep progressing toward marriage and family life with him if he wasn't aware of what the future might hold. I remember being frightened to tell him, because I knew I could lose him. I was letting him off the hook if he decided that the risk of possibly having a seriously ill child in the future was too much to ask. I loved him enough to accept that risk.

This conversation happened while we were at Lake Verna, at my parents' lake house north of Minocqua, Wisconsin. We had taken the paddleboat out for a leisurely trip around the lake at sunset. It was a gorgeous evening and we were just floating along in the summer weather, enjoying life. When we were near the boat landing opposite my parents' property, I decided to dive into the conversation with him. My bravery was fueled by a glass of wine at that point. In the Engelmeier household, we always take a beverage along on our paddleboat cruises. It's like a rule.

"Sean, I need to talk to you about something."

"Okay … what?"

He looked at me with uncertain eyes.

"So, I'm not trying to rush anything, but I also want to be realistic. We went into this about a year ago on no uncertain terms. We both said that we are done dating casually and someday want to have a family." I paused. He kept staring at me.

"So, if we were to get married and have a family one day, there is something you should know. Adrienne is a gene carrier for a rare heart condition, and both of her brothers died from it. Marty has it, but it's managed and he's doing well now. My point is, we don't know yet if I am a gene carrier and we might never know. You need to consider if you would potentially want to have a family with someone who could pass on a heart defect to your future children."

I felt my eyes well up. *Dammit, I didn't want to cry.*

Sean pulled me in close. He absorbed what I was telling him with an uncanny degree of calm and simply said, "Well, we'll cross that bridge when we come to it, honey. Even if you are a gene carrier, it's not a 100 percent certainty that our kids would have the gene. It's okay. I love you and nothing you could tell me about you would change that."

CHAPTER 11:

⤙⤙⤙

Invitation to a Funeral

In April of 2018, Adrienne asked me to accompany her on a very special visit. She wanted to meet me in Green Bay, Wisconsin, to pay a visit to her cousin Tammy.

Tammy and Adrienne were best friends throughout their childhood years. Adrienne has a sister, but she and her sister were never very close. Tammy was like the big sister that Adrienne never had.

Tammy and Adrienne were close in age. Tammy was the first of the pair to get married and have children. She was a few years older than Adrienne, and by the time I was born, she had already given birth to her first child. It was for this reason that Tammy was there to coach Adrienne through my birth, a sort of familial doula.

Adrienne and I had been reconnected for four years by the time that I was asked to meet Tammy. The reason for our meeting was less than ideal. Tammy was on her deathbed due to cancer, and one thing she wanted to check off her list was meeting the baby that she helped to bring into the world twenty-eight years before. How could I possibly say no to a request like that?

So, I made the two-hour trek to Green Bay to meet Tammy. I called Adrienne about half an hour into my drive so that she could fill me in on some of the details of Tammy's life.

Adrienne took a matter-of-fact tone. "Now, there are some things I want you to know before you step foot in Tammy's house today. First of all, you wouldn't be here if it weren't for Tammy. I mean that. She's the one who taught me how to push when I was in labor with you. She already had her firstborn by then, so she knew what she was doing. At least she knew a lot more than I did as a sixteen-year-old kid! The doctors kept saying 'bear down', and I had no idea what that meant! Then, there was Tammy who told me, 'Just push like you're takin' a shit!!' and that made all the difference! So that's the kind of person she is. She's blunt and in your face, and now that she's nearing the end of her life, she's even more so. So, I just wanted to prepare you for that."

"Also, Tammy was married, but that was a long time ago … to a man who is the father of both her kids. Well, they divorced for a lot of different reasons. But after all is said and done, she went the other way. She's been in a domestic partnership with Dorothy or, as we call her, 'Dot' for over ten years now. Dot will be there today too. So, I just wanted to prepare you for that."

It was a lot to absorb all at once. I tried to lighten the mood by telling Adrienne that all of these revelations would make for great material for my book. We shared a good laugh.

Tammy and Adrienne went through a hell of a lot together in their formative years, especially the years directly preceding and following my birth. A few months before I was born, Tammy's brother was tragically killed in a car accident. Then, after the nine months of Tammy helping Adrienne through the ups and downs of pregnancy and eventual labor and delivery, I was born. Tammy was there as Adrienne made the difficult decision to go through with the adoption. Then, less than a year after the adoption took place, in July of 1990, Adrienne's brother Allen passed away at the age of nineteen due to his undiagnosed HCM. The following year, in May, her brother Richard died at the age of twenty-one of the same disease. Tammy's divorce followed shortly after Richard's death. Tammy was Adrienne's rock and Adrienne was hers through their most challenging times in life.

The day I spent with Tammy was strange, but wonderful. Imagine meeting someone you've never known before, who is technically family, and is also dying. It was an absolute roller coaster of emotion.

Tammy was every inch the person Adrienne described her to be: brash, funny, direct, tenderhearted, and strong. We had lunch together at her house and then sat in the living room looking through boxes of family photos. Each photo felt like another tiny window into my past. I may not have been raised with the people in Adrienne's family, but I surely am part of them, as they are of me.

While Adrienne and Tammy reminisced, I felt like a door to Adrienne's childhood had been flung wide open. I studied picture after picture while listening to their stories. At one point, Dot was looking at a photo and was having trouble seeing who was in it. Like you might do to zoom in on a picture while using a smartphone, she slid her thumb and index finger across the glossy four-by-six print. We all cracked up when we realized what she had done.

The afternoon flew by and eventually Tammy was worn out. Before she retired, she looked at Adrienne and then at me. She looked me right in the eyes. "You know, I don't care how crazy this sounds. I want to personally invite you to my funeral."

I was completely taken aback. We all laughed because of the sheer absurdity of the moment.

"Well, thank you, Tammy. It really has been an honor to meet you and I will do what I can to be there."

A few weeks later, Adrienne told me that Tammy had passed away peacefully at home. My time with Tammy had been a moment when the circle of life came full circle. She was there when I was born and I was there to see her off. I'm thankful to have known her for the short time that I did.

CHAPTER 12:

⤛⤛

Bucksnort

INTERESTINGLY ENOUGH, MY BIRTH FAMILIES were the first to know about my relationship with my husband, Sean. In a roundabout way, if I had never met Todd, I never would have met Sean, the man I would one day marry and start a family with.

After I broke it off with Trent, I moved to Milwaukee to pursue my elementary education license. At that time, I held a bachelor's degree with a double major in dance and health promotion and wellness. I loved teaching dance from the age I was old enough to be a class assistant in middle school. Seeing the light bulb go on when a student understood the choreography, or just watching the dancers' faces when they were moving for the sheer love of dance, was always so rewarding to me. I spent a year focusing on teaching dance in between my college graduation and starting the elementary education program at UW–Milwaukee.

When I was in college pursuing my bachelor's degree, I felt deep satisfaction working at one of my college internships, performing community health education on the topic of breast-cancer prevention. I felt that I was doing my part to help others so that fewer women would have to suffer through what my mother had gone through. Through the scope of my internship, I was able to provide health education to more than five hundred women. I even had the chance to speak on a local radio station, where I was interviewed about the work I was doing through the Susan G. Komen Grant for the county health department.

My love of teaching and my love of children showed me that I wanted to take teaching to another level by earning my official state license and then pursuing elementary education as a fulltime career. I poured all of my energy into making my dream happen. I moved in with my best friend, Alyssa, who was well into her studies in the teaching program at UW–Milwaukee. She helped me apply for late admission into the School of Education.

I had decided to pursue teaching well before I ended things with my former fiancé, and when the breakup finally happened, I knew I needed a change of scenery, fast. I had already been accepted into UW–Madison's School of Education, but I knew I couldn't move to the same city as Trent. The Law School and School of Education were directly across the street from one another on campus. I did not want to worry about the potential for running into him day after day.

So, I decided to see what would happen if I just put feelers out into the universe. I quickly shot out a Facebook post asking if anyone near the Milwaukee or Madison areas needed summer childcare. I had a lot of valuable experience with children under my belt because of my involvement in teaching dance. I knew I would be living in Milwaukee with my best friend, but I was open to driving as far as Madison if I had to, for the right nanny gig. After all, I still hadn't officially decided where I wanted to start school in the fall, so I was flexible. Milwaukee was an option, but I knew there were other good colleges in the Milwaukee and Madison suburbs. I was still deciding what I would do.

I landed halfway between Milwaukee and Madison, in Johnson Creek. Todd's cousin, Heidi, was one of the first people to respond to my Facebook post. She and her husband were looking for summer childcare for their two children. I traveled to Johnson Creek one afternoon in late May to see if working for them would be a good fit. Everyone was sold on the idea of me becoming their summer nanny. I spent that summer commuting an hour every day to watch Heidi's children in Johnson Creek. Since they were family, I sometimes stayed overnight so that I wouldn't have to make the commute to and from Milwaukee. It was a joyful, fun-filled summer.

That summer, I felt more free than I had in my entire life. It was a strange but wonderful time for me. I spent the days running the kids ragged playing in the sun and the nights working on my applications for grad school and drinking wine with the friends I lived with. I was focused and ready for the next phase. In my heart of hearts, I prayed that God would send me my future husband as soon as possible. In my emotions, I already felt ready for marriage and a family when I had said yes to Trent, but after that crashed and burned the logical part of my brain wanted nothing to do with men and romance. I wanted to focus solely on school and my career.

God had other plans. Over the course of the summer, I came to know Heidi's neighbors, since their children and Heidi's enjoyed playing together. The more I got to know the neighbors, the more I revealed about myself. One day, I was sitting by the neighbor's pool chatting with the mom as we watched the kids swim. She knew my story by then. I had shared with her how I was ready for love if the right man came along, but that I also wasn't looking.

She began talking up her daughter's godfather, Sean. She spoke of his love for family, his work ethic, and his Catholic faith. She told me that the only reason he was single at his age (twenty-nine at the time) was because of how hard he worked. It didn't leave him much time for dating. She told me he had a house of his own and that he was a kind-hearted gentleman. She made him sound like a rare Prince Charming in what I already knew to be a dating pool full of frogs. She showed me Facebook photos of him and insisted that I let her set us up on a date. I wasn't ecstatic about it, but eventually I gave in and I let her and her boyfriend forward my phone number to Sean the mystery man. I wasn't expecting him to follow through with calling me. Everything I had heard about him sounded too good to be true.

But lo and behold, one evening he called. As the phone rang, I sat on my bed and just stared at it. I was a deer in the headlights. I didn't even have the courage to pick it up. In my mind, I knew I'd be opening a new can of worms, and I wasn't sure I wanted the headache of jumping back into the dating scene. Even talking to him could make things complicated.

What if he likes me but I'm not interested? What will our friends think if I can't stand him? What if I do end up liking him and he gets in the way of my goals and plans?

After a few minutes, I decided that I was being ridiculous and there could be no harm done from a simple phone call, so I called him back. Our conversation flowed smoothly and lasted just less than an hour. At the end of our talk, he asked if he could take me out to dinner. I accepted and he made arrangements to pick me up the following night. I kept telling myself that it was only a date and that I'd never have to see him again if it was awful. Part of me was a little anxious about having him pick me up from my house because first, I would be dependent on him for transportation and wouldn't be able to dip if I needed a way out and, second, what if he was a secret serial killer? I calmed my anxieties by telling myself that my friends would not set me up with a serial killer and that I could always sneak off to the bathroom and text my best friend Alyssa to call me and fake an emergency so I could get out of there if it was a totally disastrous date.

The night of our date, I was so nervous I almost canceled. I remember getting ready, curling my hair, and the entire time, all I could think was, *This is so stupid.* I told Alyssa that I wanted to call it off.

"Don't," she said. "You'll never get your mutual friends off your back if you don't at least go out with him once. Plus, it's a free dinner." We both laughed.

"Okay, fine you're right. It can't hurt! But have your phone on in case I need to fake an emergency and get out of there fast!"

Sean picked me up promptly at six o'clock. When the doorbell rang, I felt like I was going to pass out, or throw up, or both. All I could think was, *Why the hell am I putting myself through this?* My anxiety was overwhelming. I opened the door, and suddenly the voice I'd come to know on the phone had a very handsome face attached to it. Seeing Sean for the first time actually took my breath away.

"Hi, Lori?" Sean asked. It was a completely blind date for him. He didn't even Facebook stalk beforehand.

"Yep, that's me!"

We were so drawn to each other that we hugged right away. Sean walked me to the car and opened the door for me, impressing me with his gentlemanly ways.

We enjoyed a romantic dinner at a small local restaurant followed by an impromptu trip to Dave and Buster's arcade. All in all, it was a great night. Sean was sweet, funny, and enjoyable to be around. By the end of our first date, I knew I liked Sean much, much more than I wanted to.

The next night, after some pressure from the couple who had set us up, I called Sean for a second date. It was really forward of me, but I also knew that I had nothing to lose. We went to a late-night movie and we were the only ones in the theater. We sat and talked the entire time. Neither of us could tell you what that movie was about.

After that, I let things cool off for a few weeks before grad school started, but our conversations were growing deeper, and I knew I wanted to see him again soon. I decided to invite him to a Kurth-family camping event to celebrate the end of summer. A Kurth event is like nothing you have ever experienced in your life unless you've lived in the Wisconsin Northwoods. The Kurths were camping with a few other families at a little campground in Tripoli, Wisconsin, called Bucksnort. The resort's end-of-summer bash was the weekend of the Kurth camping extravaganza, and there was a band playing every night at the campground bar along with daily beanbag tournaments and a pig roast. It was the perfect way to close out the season.

Sean worked all day on Friday of that weekend, and then made the four-and-a-half-hour trek up to Bucksnort to join in on the family fun with me. By the time he arrived after midnight, we were all half in the bag. We had been drinking most of the evening by that point and engaging in a ceremonial burning of my Save-the-Date cards, which were supposed to be sent out for my wedding to Trent around that time, had we stayed together. It was cathartic, throwing the cards into the fire while surrounded by my family and friends. Everyone grabbed a handful and watched the colors burn. There were strangers I didn't even know throwing them into the fire by the handful and cheering for me. I needed to destroy those very tangible fragments of my past life in order to move forward. It was a beautifully therapeutic, controlled act of pyromania.

After Sean arrived around midnight, he stayed up for an hour or so with us and had a beer. Then, right before everyone turned in for the night, Sean and I shared our first kiss. He had made attempts at a chaste peck on the lips on both of our previous dates, but I always ducked his advances, knowing it would have only escalated my feelings for him. It would have given the relationship more weight, in my mind. This time, I let him kiss me goodnight, and I knew that what I felt in that moment was going to continue to spiral into something deeper. After the kiss goodnight, I laughed out loud.

"What?" he asked, taken aback.

"I can't believe our first kiss was a drunk goodnight kiss while I'm wearing my retainer," I said.

"Well, whatever. It's fine," Sean said with a shrug and a smile.

It mattered greatly to me that Sean received unanimous approval from my family. That weekend was his chance to prove himself, and he definitely did. Sean was well-liked by Todd, Jamie, and the girls. I knew at that point that I wanted more from our relationship than the friendship we had already built. I made arrangements to meet Sean where he lived in Waukesha the following week.

It was a hot summer night in August when I drove to Waukesha. When I arrived at Sean's house, the weather was perfect for a stroll under the stars. We went out to the Fox River Parkway and walked hand in hand down the meandering path. I am not known to beat around the bush and I was tired of our undefined relationship status. So, I pointedly asked Sean, "Where is this going?"

As a joke, he began to describe the ins and outs of the Fox River Parkway that we were walking on.

"No". I said. "Us ... you and me."

There was a pause and then he said, "Well … I'd like you to be my girlfriend."

And I responded with, "Good. 'Cause I want you to be my boyfriend." It was comically juvenile, but also very sweet. From that day forward, we were on our journey toward the altar, though we didn't know it at first.

The day after Sean and I decided on our official relationship status, I met Adrienne for a visit. I sat across from her at the table in the restaurant where we were having lunch, still finding it so strange and surreal that I had a boyfriend. She was fully supportive and told me she wanted nothing more than for me to be happy. She told me she felt similar the first time she dated someone after her split with Mitch. I was worried that it was too soon to be seeing someone, and she told me just to take it slow and enjoy the moment. Not only did my birth mother help me out of my previous toxic relationship, she helped me ease me into the start of a new, healthy relationship.

At that time of my life, I wanted the approval of my birth parents first before introducing Sean to my parents. I was living at home when I went through my breakup with Trent, and my parents witnessed the carnage firsthand. It was as hard on them to see their only daughter going through some of the worst pain of her life as it was on me experiencing it. I wanted to be sure of what I was doing before including them in the equation, and Todd and Adrienne were my go-to people for an honest first impression. My confidence in my own judgment was somewhat tarnished after having almost married the wrong man. I put a great deal of stock in the opinions of my family to help me see the truth.

Naturally, my parents were skeptical at first when I told them I had a new boyfriend. It also may have had something to do with the fact that Sean's Facebook profile picture at the time was a photo of him smoking a hookah. Not the greatest first impression. But, Sean spent his Labor Day weekend at the Engelmeier family lake house with us that summer and began to win them over. There was no shortage of Sean being grilled by my father that first night. He put Sean on the spot with every question he could think of, from asking him about his career to his views on politics, to his family background. Sean handled the inquisition with confidence and grace. Immediately, my dad liked Sean's work ethic and my mother admired his honesty and sense of humor. My father is a difficult man to impress and sometimes even a difficult man to converse with, but somehow Sean managed to accomplish both things at once. By the end of the weekend, Sean had begun to win their hearts.

School began after Labor Day, and I spent every weekend at Sean's house with him. With the start of the school year, I had taken a new job as a live-in nanny for a family with two sets of twins. I was essentially working whenever I wasn't in night class. It was a very demanding time. I had weekends off, and by Friday night every week, I was more than ready to get away. I adored the family I worked for, but I needed space too. Sean graciously let me stay with him all weekend, every weekend, even though we had only been together a few weeks at that point. It wasn't a matter of wanting every second of his time, just an escape from my hectic reality. It gave me the peace I needed to accomplish schoolwork and relax with Sean as we got to know each other. My life felt so strange and uncertain at that time, like I was coming into a new skin that I never knew lay underneath. Sean was a part of that metamorphosis.

The author F. Scott Fitzgerald once described a romance by saying,

"They slipped briskly into an intimacy from which they never recovered."

This perfectly describes the relationship that Sean and I progressed into. We fell unexpectedly and quickly in love. Our first year of dating flew by in the blink of an eye. We shared a lot of everyday loveliness as well as some big milestones along the way. Sean took me to Kentucky to spend Thanksgiving with his parents that year. Later on, in January, he took me to Seattle for a week to spend some time with his brother. We went on countless dinner dates, attended a few Milwaukee Brewers baseball games, spent time getting to know each other's friends and families, and made our way through a few big arguments that tested our relationship. Sean celebrated his thirtieth birthday ten months after we started dating, and I managed to throw him a surprise birthday party that was well-attended by family and friends. Our first year set the tone for our relationship: adventure, compromise, shared values, and love. We knew what we shared was meaningful and we both hoped for a bright future together.

CHAPTER 13:

⤜⤜

The Next Destination

I WAS CLEAR ABOUT MY hopes for our relationship on my twenty-sixth birthday, in October of 2015. I pointed out to Sean that I was officially closer to being thirty than I was to being twenty.

"Well, I want to have my first child no later than age thirty, which means I need to be married no later than age twenty-nine. But, I always wanted to be married for at least a year before having kids, so that brings it down to age twenty-eight. And it takes a year to plan a wedding."

Sean is the type of person who likes to take his time and weigh the pros and cons of every situation. He had always said he'd never live with someone before getting married, because he'd been burned by that situation in the past. He would just get married. I reminded him that I'd be graduating and ready to move out of my junky college apartment in a year, which would be another reason to consider marriage. I thought it was downright stupid to continue living separate lives, as involved as we had become.

Our second year of dating was full of just as many adventures as the first. We took a trip to Antigua in the Bahamas to celebrate Sean's parents' thirty-fifth wedding anniversary, a vacation to Las Vegas with Sean's brother and his girlfriend, a Wisconsin River canoe trip where the two of us weathered a violent thunderstorm followed by a scorching heat wave, and we navigated many other adventures as well as ups and downs. In the end, we always seemed to come out stronger and more in love, no matter what tested us.

My twenty-seventh birthday was my unofficial ultimatum for Sean. I had put it in no uncertain terms that if we weren't taking the next step in our relationship by then, after nearly two and a half years of dating, then there would be some reconsideration to do. I am not one to waste my time. I did enough of that in the past with my ex-fiancé. And I had never felt about Trent or anyone else the way I felt about Sean.

We looked at engagement rings together in August of 2017, several months before my birthday. October came and I hadn't seen a ring in Sean's possession. I had no idea if one would be making an appearance around the time of my birthday.

I decided it would be fun to visit Sean's parents in Kentucky for my birthday weekend. The horse track was open that time of year, and I had always wanted to dress up and attend the races. I was on edge all weekend, wondering if perhaps a racetrack proposal was in order, or even a proposal somewhere along our road trip.

I had stayed up late the night before Sean and I left, drinking wine to celebrate my birthday with my college roommate. Unfortunately, I was feeling the effects of it the next day and it made me late to meet Sean to leave on our road trip. Little did I know that this lateness was going to cost me my coveted proposal! The drive to Kentucky would take us nine hours, and we were already leaving at five p.m. instead of our earlier planned time of three p.m. He didn't want to hold us up any longer. Later, I found out that Sean had been planning to propose right then and there before we hit the road by placing the ring on the front seat of the vehicle while I was packing up, and then getting down on one knee when I opened the door and saw it there. Instead, he hung onto the ring all weekend, hatching a new plan of action.

The week after my birthday, I was going absolutely crazy. When we returned home from our Kentucky weekend, I was unpacking Sean's duffel bag. Out fell a bag from Kessler's, the place for diamonds in Southeastern Wisconsin. Once I realized what I was most likely holding, I dropped it on the bed like a hot potato and let out a little yelp. I didn't open it, but I knew in my heart what it was. I couldn't let on that I knew and cost Sean his pride. So, I did my best to wait patiently. Sean called me up one night and asked if I wanted to go out to dinner the following night, a Thursday. It was a bit out of the ordinary for Sean to take me out on a weeknight, but it wasn't like we hadn't gone out to eat on a weeknight before, so I tried not to think too much of it. Sean picked me up and we went to Balzac, a small-plates bistro on Milwaukee's east side.

As we pulled up to the parking lot at the restaurant, Sean asked me to jump out and look at the meter to see how much change we needed. He used this moment to hide the ring on the front seat under his coat. I was oblivious.

We enjoyed a delicious dinner and cocktails and we were walking back to the vehicle when a rough-looking stranger started chatting us up in the parking lot. Unfortunately, the area around the restaurant had recently become one of the major homeless hangouts in Milwaukee, with street bums often following people to their vehicles asking for money. I was instantly on high alert, and Sean and I power-walked to the car with the stranger following us about ten paces behind. I whipped open the door and jumped into the vehicle.

"Lock the doors!" I demanded as Sean got in.

It was then that I realized I was sitting on something. I pulled Sean's coat out from under me and the box with the ring went flying to the floor. I was stunned. I thought Sean had forgotten he'd placed the ring there. It seemed like a careless mistake to leave the ring sitting in a heap with his coat on the front seat of the car. As I found out in that instant, it was no mistake at all.

I looked over at Sean and saw a look in his eyes that I had never seen there before.

"Lori," he said.

"Oh my god. Is this for real?" I asked.

"Yes," he continued.

"Lori. You make me the happiest I've ever been in my life. I want to walk through the great unknown with you by my side. Lori Ann Engelmeier, would you do me the incredible honor of being my wife?"

I was shaking from head to toe. I was crying. I was laughing. I was having what Sean would later describe as a happy panic attack. I said "Yes," with every fiber of my being.

The next few days were an excited flurry as we told all our family and friends the big news. Everyone was thrilled and overjoyed for us. Happy moments such as this one had become infinitely more joyful since acquiring two more sets of parents and families to share them with. I couldn't wait for the journey to come.

CHAPTER 14:

꜊꜊꜊

The Wedding

IN JANUARY OF 2017, RIGHT after Sean and I got engaged, we went to Wisconsin Rapids to visit Adrienne and Daryl. My best friend Alyssa came with us, along with my cousin Casie, who is Adrienne's niece. I am lucky enough to call Casie one of my very best friends. We clicked the day we met and we've been inseparable ever since. We arrived in Wisconsin Rapids in the late afternoon and we were all having a drink and catching up. Both Alyssa and Casie had agreed to stand up in my wedding, and, of course, talk of the wedding and excitement for the big day came up. Suddenly, you could see the wheels start turning with all of us girls. I'm sure Daryl and Sean thought, *Lord, help us.*

Adrienne asked if I had a theme or color scheme in mind for the big day. I told her that I was playing with the idea of a sparkly winter wonderland, since our date was set for December 30, 2017.

"Well, you know …" she said. "Why don't we just go out shopping and see what kind of after-Christmas deals are going on right now? If we find anything, you can keep it here and bring it home for the big day later."

The four of us girls lit up like a Christmas tree. All of us working together basically cleared out Wal-mart's holiday section. We found dozens of blue-and-silver wintry decorations that were perfect for a winter wonderland theme, yet not too Christmassy. We came up with the idea of creating sparkling customized ornaments for wedding favors from clear ornament bulbs we found on the shelves. Each of us had a cart full of décor by the time we made our way through the holiday sale aisles.

When we got to the checkouts, Adrienne pulled me aside. "Now, I am going to cover this. I won't, though, if you think Mom and Dad would be offended. I don't want to step on any toes. But I never thought in my whole life that I'd get to help with your big day, and this is the least I can do if you'll let me."

And there we were, getting emotional in the middle of a Wal-mart in Wisconsin Rapids. I assured Adrienne that her gift was much appreciated and that my parents wouldn't be offended at all by her generosity. It was the first of many more times that I would feel the beauty of the surreal experience of planning my wedding with my birth mother's help.

As the wedding planning progressed, Adrienne became absolutely invaluable. She has been a professional event planner for years. In her spare time, she puts on regular fundraisers and banquets for local groups, and she planned many events as a baseball mom over the years. She planned her own wedding reception for more than 500 people. When it came to my wedding, no detail went unnoticed. We had daily conference calls to discuss wedding planning items as the big day got closer and closer.

Adrienne helped me handle it all: the reception décor, the church décor, the flowers, the seating charts, dealing with the caterer, and situations that arose with groomsmen, bridesmaids, or family members. She had an answer and idea for every question or obstacle on the wedding-planning path. She worked in tandem with my mother, always questioning whether or not she was overstepping her role. She didn't want to intrude on my mom and I, but both my mom and I know that if it weren't for Adrienne, the whole process would have been a lot more stressful for everyone involved. My mother is not an event planner, and she and I probably would have gone insane trying to coordinate it all while living in separate cities and learning all we needed to learn about planning a huge formal event at the same time. Adrienne was our godsend.

One afternoon about ten months before the date of the wedding, my mom and I went to visit Adrienne. Adrienne had met with an events company to see about securing decor rentals for the reception. She wanted to show my mom and I the catalog of decor we could choose from if we wanted to. She also wanted to have a sit down with both of us to make absolutely certain that we were comfortable with the role she had taken on helping to plan the wedding.

We sat in Adrienne's entertaining area in her beautiful home, thumbing through the pages of the catalog, becoming more and more excited with all that we saw. Adrienne launched into her speech then and there. "Now, I know that this is a very special time for mothers and daughters. I want you both to be 100-percent comfortable with everything I have done so far, or anything I could help with in the future. I don't want to intrude on any of this for both of you. I'm just here to help if you need it."

My mom got misty-eyed, and then so did I.

"Adrienne," Mom said. "I wouldn't even be a mom if it weren't for you! You are our godsend! I don't have an event-planning bone in my body!"

We all laughed. It was settled, then!

When the wedding day finally arrived, the event itself was the catalyst for all of my birth families to bury the hatchet of years gone by. It was a beautiful testament to the power of love and forgiveness.

Todd and Adrienne went through a rocky end to their relationship years ago. They hadn't spoken in more than twenty years and they both had anxiety about attending the wedding and seeing each other. Adrienne sincerely felt that Todd owed her an apology for the way he treated her in the past, and Todd knew it, too. I remember talking over Adrienne's anxieties with her. I offered to pass her contact information along to Todd and leave the ball in his court. After a few months of me continually suggesting this, Adrienne relented. Essentially, I was sick of seeing her worry and not do anything to alleviate the situation. Todd was also anxious about being at an event with Adrienne. Neither he nor Adrienne wanted a big scene, but they knew that a lot had changed in the past twenty-eight years and that they'd have to face the music and put the past in the past sooner or later.

One summer night in June of 2017, I was sitting in Todd's kitchen with him and Jamie. My sixteen-year-old sister, Morgan, was also there. Todd and I were a few beers into our evening (imagine that) and the topic of the wedding and Adrienne arose. The drinks made me more loose-lipped than I usually am and I told Todd in no uncertain terms that Adrienne felt that she was owed an apology for whatever happened between them.

"I don't know what happened and I don't want to know. But what I do want is for this wedding to be a celebration of love and a day of fun for all my family and friends. You probably can't get away without having at least one conversation with her at the wedding, so think of it this way. You could crack a beer, sit down on your deck that overlooks the woods and give her a call, or you could wait until the biggest day of my life when you're already going to have a million emotions going through your head."

"Exactly, Kurth Guy," Jamie said, using her pet name for Todd.

Morgan sat back and smiled, just taking everything in. She liked being privy to our adult conversations and she was mature enough to handle them at her age.

The night of the wedding rehearsal arrived on December 29, 2017. Todd had never reached out to Adrienne, and consequently they had not broken their more than twenty-year silence.

Naturally, I was a nervous wreck the night before my wedding. My perfectionist personality was on overdrive, my excitement was through the roof, and my anxiety was firing like crazy. I was thirty minutes late to my own wedding rehearsal because I was so delirious on raw emotion that we literally drove past the church three times while looking for it. There was also a heavy, wet snow falling lightly, turning everything into a slippery wonderland of white and, to be fair, the entrance was not well-marked, making it hard to see in the dark. I texted Adrienne to let her know I was running late and asked her to have people start working on pew bows and other décor. She is experienced in rallying troops. She recruited a few of her own family members to start working on décor while everyone else enjoyed each other's company.

The dinner that followed the rehearsal at the church put everyone in jovial spirits. Months after the wedding, I found out that it was Morgan who had broken the ice between Todd and Adrienne that evening before the wedding. She must have been listening intently back in their kitchen on that summer night in June. She was standing at the buffet line and saw Adrienne on her way up to the bar. Morgan made a beeline for her.

"Hi, Adrienne!"

Adrienne was delighted to see her. Adrienne had previously met Morgan and Brianna at my wedding shower in October, and both girls loved her.

Immediately, Morgan pulled her over toward Todd and Jamie. "Come and say hi to everybody!"

It didn't leave anyone a choice. Morgan had forcibly broken the ice the way only a headstrong yet well-meaning sixteen year old can. A few minutes of small talk passed between Adrienne, Todd, and Todd's family. The much-anticipated first meeting had happened. It was time to let go and focus on enjoying the wedding day.

In addition to the Todd–Adrienne situation, there was the Kurth/Schultz question mark. Todd's parents divorced when he was a young child and his mother remarried later on. Todd still has a strong relationship with his birth father, Wayne Schultz, and the rest of his Schultz family. The rest of the Kurth family pretty much stopped interacting with the Schultzes after the divorce. There was bad blood between Todd's mother and her former husband for many years. Todd was the only one who had kept contact, and because of this I had met and come to love the Schultz family as well. Todd's birth father, his wife, and Todd's half sister were all in attendance at my wedding.

Our wedding would be the first time that Todd's mom and biological father would be in the same room for the same reason in more than twenty years. If they were worried about crossing paths, neither one of them ever expressed this concern to me. Todd's biological father mentioned to Jamie, Todd's wife, that he was considering not coming because he didn't want to cause any trouble. Jamie encouraged him to come and not worry about it at all. She made it clear that he and his family were wanted and they would be missed if they decided not to come. Even before the wedding day took place, the event itself was becoming a force of nature, causing people to consider letting go of old hurts they had been clinging to for years.

The day of the wedding, everyone seemed to radiate joy and love. Everyone danced their hearts out at the reception and the love was tangible in the air. My father gave the most sentimental father-of-the-bride speech you have ever heard, and he made special mention of Todd and Adrienne.

"I would like to recognize Todd and Adrienne," he said with a pointed glance into the crowd, "who are here in attendance, the birthparents of our daughter. Were it not for their commitment to life, and the love of their baby, and the sacrifice of adoption, this day would not have occurred." Although he had started to press forward in his speech, the room erupted in applause, recognizing the incredible melding of two worlds that was taking place as the result of our wedding.

I was so anxious about every last detail of the day that I didn't let loose until the last hour or so of the reception. Then I decided it was time to let everything go and just drink the wine we had already paid for as I danced the night away with my husband and our friends. After the reception, Sean and I walked down the street to our favorite bar, surrounded by friends and family. Well, Sean walked. He carried me so that my wedding dress wouldn't drag through the snow. It was December 30 in Wisconsin, after all.

After the bar closed down, we all made our way across the street to the hotel. Up in her hotel room, Adrienne laid out an absolute feast of smoked meats, cheeses, crackers, and dips. As everyone talked and laughed, I paused for a moment to take it all in. Daryl and Todd were talking shop about smoking meats in one corner of the room. Adrienne and I were snacking together, and my sister Morgan, Jamie, my best friend Alyssa, and my sister Brianna were all in the mix too. Never in a million years would I have imagined that my wedding night would look like it did, celebrating with all of my birth families and my family who raised me, all under one roof!

My half brother Ben was an usher for the ceremony and he escorted my mom down the aisle. My two half sisters were bridesmaids. Adrienne's niece, Casie, was also a bridesmaid. And of course, Adrienne was the event-planning mastermind behind that special day.

One afternoon, after the wedding, Adrienne and I were catching up.

"Never would I have dared to dream that it would be my son walking your mom down the aisle or that I'd even be a part of your wedding day," she said. We both got emotional then.

It was truly a moment in time when life came full circle. Our wedding was like the happy ending of a fairy tale. Everyone I spoke to on and after that day commented on how much tangible love was felt in the room the entire day and night. I will forever cherish my wedding day as the day of new beginnings, not only for Sean and I but also for all the people we love the most.

CHAPTER 15:

꧁

Our Family Is Growing by Two Little Feet!

I WILL NEVER FORGET THE week I found out that I was pregnant with our first child. Sean and I had just returned from a whirlwind weekend trip to Seattle. Sean's brother, Mike, had married his wife, Rachel at a beautiful country club in the Pacific Northwest. Sean and I were both members of the wedding party. It was a joyful weekend filled with fun, laughter, and family.

As soon as we arrived in Seattle, we made a run to the grocery store. I think it was the third quart of yogurt I placed in the cart that was the tipping point for Sean. "We're only going to be here for three days! Are you really going to eat that much yogurt?!" I was starving. I did eat most of it before the trip was over. Sean scarfed the last bits of leftovers before we departed for the airport on our last day.

On the day before the wedding, the wedding rehearsal was held outdoors. The weather was unseasonably warm for Seattle that July, and I remember feeling as if I were melting in the hot summer sun. Sweat poured down my back and I couldn't wait to get back into the comfort of the air-conditioned indoors. I felt like I was dying of heat exhaustion and thirst. I know that sounds dramatic, but that is truly how I felt! Anyone who knows me knows that I don't tolerate the heat well.

As soon as we arrived at the restaurant for the rehearsal dinner, I downed glass after glass of water. While I mingled with the wedding party and our family members who were all in town for the wedding, Sean had a moment alone with his brother. When you're the most recently married couple in the family, as Sean and I were, everyone always wants to know the answer to one question. "When are you having kids?"

"So, Sean … Rachel and I noticed that Lori's drinking water tonight …. Does that mean anything in particular?" Mike asked with a twinkle in his eye.

Sean laughed. "No it doesn't … Well, no, not that either of us know of!"

The day of the wedding arrived and it could not have been a more perfect summer day. The wedding was beautiful. I, however, was starving and exhausted all weekend. I was so tired that I accidentally slept through my alarm and was late for work the day after we came home! Five days later, I found out that I was pregnant. It all made sense: The hunger, the exhaustion in the heat, the insatiable thirst. I was shocked and overjoyed, since it was literally the first month that we had been trying to conceive.

I wanted to surprise Sean and tell him the news in a unique way. However, I am terrible at keeping surprises a secret for any length of time. He already knew that my period was late and he called me on his break from work to check in.

"So, did you do the test?"

"Uh-huh," I said, unable to keep the smile from my voice.

"Well?" he said.

"We're having a baby!" I exclaimed.

"Oh honey. That's great! I love you!"

We were absolutely over the moon. Our dreams for a future filled with children were beginning to take shape. We couldn't wait to meet our baby in just nine short months.

CHAPTER 16:

⤙⤙⤙

You're Going to Be a Grandparent!

EVERYONE WE SHARED THE NEWS with was ecstatic when we told them we were expecting. It was such a thrill to share the special announcement with our families. Our baby would be the first grandchild for both Sean's parents and mine, as well as Todd and Jamie!

My favorite reaction to our announcement came when I told Todd's family. Todd, Jamie, and my sisters came to stay with us for Labor Day weekend. My sister Morgan wanted to start the visit by raiding my closet for a dress she could wear to homecoming. I was only too happy to oblige, since I never had the chance to experience these kinds of sisterly bonding moments growing up. Morgan and I were chatting away and she was rifling through dress after dress in my closet when all of a sudden, she went dead silent.

"Lori?! …" she said, her voice rising an octave.

I had totally forgotten that I'd stashed some baby clothes in the closet the week before, complete with the tags still on them. There was Morgan, holding up a onesie staring at me with huge, expectant eyes.

"Shit. You weren't supposed to find that." I smiled and snatched it from her.

She started jumping up and down with sheer elation and squealing.

"Shhh, shh!!" I said. "You have to keep it together! I wanted to tell everyone all at once before dinner!"

A few minutes later, after Morgan had calmed down, we walked downstairs to the kitchen to rejoin the group. I was sure that our faces were going to give us away, but everyone was having a great time socializing and tipping back some beers.

"Did you find a dress?" Jamie asked Morgan.

"Yep!" she replied with a laugh. I laughed too. We both knew she had found so much more than that!

"Lori, grab a drink and join us!"

Thankfully, I was prepared. I had a tumbler cup full of water on the ready.

"Did you see my tumbler down here? I don't remember where I put it. I mixed something right before you guys came."

Todd grabbed it off of the counter and handed it to me. "Here you go, Sunshine."

"Thanks. Why don't we all go sit out on the patio for a bit? It's such a nice night."

I grabbed some gifts I had wrapped for Todd, Jamie, and the girls. Morgan's birthday was in July and Brianna's was in August, so I was going to play it off like they were belated birthday gifts. They were actually pregnancy announcements.

"So I know it's a little belated, but I have some birthday gifts for the girls, and something small for you guys, Todd and Jamie, just because."

I could barely contain my smile as I handed them the gifts.

"What?" Jamie said. "You shouldn't have gotten us anything." She unwrapped the gift and inside was a countdown-until-we're-grandparents calendar. The instant the realization dawned on her, she threw the calendar into the air and shrieked, wrapping me up in a giant hug and jumping up and down.

Morgan was laughing because she knew already, Todd was tearing up, and Brianna was smiling, totally dumbfounded as she stared at the best-auntie-ever t-shirt she had just unwrapped. It was a moment to cherish forever.

In October, I celebrated my twenty-ninth birthday. It was the first time that I spent my birthday with Todd. That had not happened since the day I was born, twenty-nine years earlier. The weekend of my birthday, Todd and Jamie had been at a wedding in Chicago and they stayed with us in Waukesha to break up their trek back home. My mother-in-law was visiting at the time, and she made a delicious home-cooked meal and birthday cake for the occasion. As we sat around the table enjoying each other's company, I asked Todd if he remembered any of the details about the day I was born ... if anything in particular stood out in his mind. Just being able to sit there with him and ask that question on my birthday was like a lifelong dream coming true. He was honest and confessed that he didn't remember much. He told me that in light of things, it was actually a very sad and difficult time for him, grappling with the finality of the decision of adoption. I, like Todd, have a knack for blocking out particularly painful periods in my life. For example, I don't remember a lot of 2012, the year that my mom went through her second bout of cancer and Sally died. Things got very emotional very quickly, as Todd was telling me about the difficulty he experienced surrounding my birth. He knew it was the right decision, but it broke his heart in two.

Pat, my mother in law chimed in to break up the heaviness of the moment.

"I think that adoption is the most selfless thing a person can do, especially when so many others don't even choose to give a baby a chance at life. I commend you and Adrienne for making such a tough call, especially at such a young age."

Todd, Jamie, Pat, and I all got a little misty eyed then. Sean was the only one who remained cool as a cucumber.

"Great, now we're all crying," I laughed. "Except for Sean!"

"You should have seen me when the equipment broke down at work last week!" Sean joked, ever the comic relief. We moved on to talking about what my birth experience would be like. Todd and Jamie asked if we had decided whether or not we wanted to know the sex of our baby before it was born.

"I want to know, and Sean doesn't want to know. So we're compromising and finding out," I joked with them.

"You could do a fun little gender reveal just the two of you … ." Jamie said. "Something to make it special and still have that element of surprise but also to help you plan … I know!!!" she said, and smacked her palms down on the table to emphasize her excitement. "Here's what you can do! Tell the ultrasound tech you don't want to know the sex. Have them write it down and put it in an envelope. Then send the envelope to me and I'll send a package with either boy or girl stuff for you guys to open together!"

The next day I called my mom and asked if she and my dad would be comfortable with that. After all, it meant that Todd and Jamie would know the sex of our baby before anyone else did. I didn't want my parents to feel slighted in any way. My mother doesn't have a jealous or competitive bone in her body.

"Oh, I think that's a great idea!" she gushed, when I told her about Jamie's suggestion. It was settled then. Todd and Jamie would be instrumental in our gender reveal!

A few weeks later, in early November, my mom came to Waukesha for my first ultrasound appointment. Never having been pregnant herself, the experience was just as magical for her as it was for me. We both cried the instant we saw that little human dancing around inside of me. It was truly surreal. My dream of becoming a mom was happening, and my mom was there to see it. The enormity of that moment was not lost on me. There were times during her cancer treatments when we were both scared that she wouldn't be there for her future grandbabies.

My ultrasound took place on a Friday. I was planning on putting the envelope with the baby's sex in the mail as soon as I got home, which meant it would go out on Saturday and reach Todd and Jamie in Minocqua by Monday or Tuesday. After the excitement of seeing my little one on the ultrasound screen, my mom looked at me and said, "Can we go to the post office today?" So we did, and we sent it by express mail. We were both eager to know what baby Williams would be!

One afternoon, I was talking with my mom on the phone, as I tend to do multiple times a week. Happy? Call Mom. Sad? Call Mom. Need advice? Call Mom. Bored? Call Mom. You get the picture. This particular conversation took place between the date of my first ultrasound and when we would find out the baby's gender. My mother is a deeply spiritual woman who taught me to see the divine in the everyday. She started off our conversation by saying, "I have to tell you about the coolest God Sighting I experienced at church on Sunday."

"Go on!" I said. She and I live for these moments when we can share these spiritual connections with each other.

She told me that the gospel for that day was an excerpt from the book of Matthew. It was the parable of the workers in the vineyard.

"For the kingdom of heaven is like a landowner who went out early in the morning to hire workers for his vineyard. He agreed to pay them a wage for the day and sent them into his vineyard.

"About nine in the morning he went out and saw others standing in the marketplace doing nothing. He told them, 'You also go and work in my vineyard, and I will pay you whatever is right.' So they went.

"He went out again about noon and about three in the afternoon and did the same thing. About five in the afternoon he went out and found still others standing around. He asked them, 'Why have you been standing here all day long doing nothing?'

"'Because no one has hired us,' they answered.

"He said to them, 'You also go and work in my vineyard.'

"When evening came, the owner of the vineyard said to his fore-man, 'Call the workers and pay them their wages, beginning with the last ones hired and going on to the first.'

"The workers who were hired about five in the afternoon came and each received their wage. So when those came who were hired first, they expected to receive more. But each one of them also received the same. When they received it, they began to grumble against the landowner. 'These who were hired last worked only one hour,' they said, 'and you have made them equal to us who have borne the burden of the work and the heat of the day.'

"But he answered one of them, 'I am not being unfair to you, friend. Didn't you agree to work for this wage? Take your pay and go. I want to give the one who was hired last the same as I gave you. Don't I have the right to do what I want with my own money? Or are you envious because I am generous?'

"So the last will be first, and the first will be last." (Matthew, 20:1–16, NIV)

Although the meaning can sometimes be complicated, there are many ways that this parable applies to my experience with adoption. My mother phrased it something like this, "When you were born, Todd and Adrienne kept you for a legally allowed ten-day waiting period. After giving birth to you, Adrienne had second thoughts about going through with the adoption and I can't blame her one bit. I had already quit my job and I was ready to stay at home with you and be your mom. Those ten days felt like an eternity of waiting. In those first days of your life, Adrienne and Todd were the first to hold you, feed you, see your first baby smiles. Now twenty-nine years have passed and I'm so grateful to be your mom and that you've been able to reconnect with both your birth parents."

"As I heard this gospel parable," Mom continued, "I was sitting there in church thinking of Todd. He was the first to be there when your life began … and I know from talking with Jamie that the years before you reconnected were very hard on him. Even after our adoption agreement to send letters and pictures for the first five years of your life expired, he requested that we stay in touch and keep sending him updates on you if we were comfortable with it. And of course, we were. Now, his first child is about to have his first grandbaby. And who is the first to know what this precious baby will be, boy or girl? Todd! He spent years being the last to know of what was happening in your life, so to speak, and now you are giving him the honor of being the first to share in the joy of knowing whether your precious baby is a little boy or girl. After all the years of pain and wondering about his daughter, this must be such a joyous occasion for him. I think it's just wonderful for you to include him in this in the way that you are! What a gift!"

Cue. The. Tears.

"Mom, I couldn't be more grateful that Todd and Adrienne chose you and Dad for my parents! So many parents might feel slighted or jealous because of my relationship with my birth parents, but you have always been supportive and for that I am so incredibly grateful!"

And then as if she couldn't imagine it being any other way, my mother said, "Well of course I'm supportive! If it weren't for Todd and Adrienne, I would never have had the chance to be a mom, your mom. What they did was the greatest gift anyone could have ever given me."

(Note: As I sat there writing this, my eyes were welling up with big, fat, pregnant tears of emotion.) I am telling you, my mother truly is a saint. And so are Todd and Adrienne for that matter, for making the choice that they did.

Let me tell you about an additional way that this scripture applies to adoption. My parents who raised me are my parents, 100 percent. My dad walked me down the aisle on my wedding day and my mom is forever the first person who comes to mind when I hear the word "mother." It would be weird to start calling Adrienne "Mom" or Todd "Dad." In light of these facts, here is how this scripture is relevant.

Adrienne and Todd are like the workers who came at the end of the day. They are putting in their time now, growing a relationship with me. Even though they weren't there during my early formative years, they have been a part of my life for my formative adult years. Even though they didn't put in the work of raising me, they are no less entitled to a relationship with me than my own parents are, because without them, my parents would not be my parents. My parents put in the long years of raising me: sensitive, stubborn, passionate, emotional, loving, and strong-willed person that I am. But Todd and Adrienne put in the long years of wondering and wishing and hoping the best for that sensitive, stubborn, passionate, emotional, loving, and strong-willed baby that they created but never got to meet until she was all grown up. In a way, my parents raised me to adulthood, and my birth parents raised me through adulthood.

As I've mentioned before, I met Todd at a tumultuous time in my early twenties. His love and acceptance helped to guide me out of a dark place and filled a part of my soul that had been empty for years. I met Adrienne just before another trying time in my life, and her guidance and love kept me from making the biggest mistake of my life—marrying the wrong man. I turned to them then, and I still turn to my birth parents now when I need advice without judgment. I know that they've been through hell and back and that I can count on them for honesty and compassion in the face of my own choices or life's simple roadblocks.

When it comes to my own parents, I could never speak so freely to them about some of the questionable choices I made along the way in my twenties. They see the little girl they raised into a woman, and this lens often frames how they see the situation. Adrienne and Todd see the woman they've known since she was an early twenty-something, blossoming into the fuller version of herself. They also see traits of themselves in me that account for both my good and bad choices, and they understand some of my best and worst decisions more clearly because of this. This is the beauty of our relationship. It is definitely familial in its warmth and loyalty, but it's more like having an aunt and uncle or older siblings to rely on, rather than being accountable to the mother and father who raised you.

Now that I have a family of my own, my children will never know a life without four sets of amazing grandparents. They will never have to wonder about their family history or feel that sense of incompleteness that I did growing up. All the cards are out on the table, and together we make a full house.

CHAPTER 17:

❧

The Gender Reveal
and its Impact

LESS THAN A WEEK AFTER I sent off Baby Williams' ultrasound to Todd and Jamie, a package arrived on our front doorstep. They had gone above and beyond and used a courier service to ship our gender-reveal package to us as quickly as possible.

I sat on the couch next to Sean, my heart pounding, as we opened the package together. Out popped a helium balloon with the inscription, "It's a Boy!"

Sean and I both experienced a crazy cocktail of emotions at that moment Of course, we couldn't have been happier to know that we would have a son. We were both looking forward to giving the baby a pronoun, instead of constantly referring to our developing fetus as "it." On the other hand, we knew there were very real risks associated with the baby's sex. So far, it had seemed that only boys inherited the gene for hypertrophic cardiomyopathy (HCM), the disease that killed both of Adrienne's brothers. We did not yet know whether or not I was a carrier of the gene.

Enter my father, Richard Engelmeier, the one man in central Wisconsin with vast knowledge on this cardiac condition. The second we knew that my baby was a boy, Dad was lining up testing with a genetics lab. He had done his research and already knew which lab would be the best for handling this type of scenario.

In my teenage years, my father had looked into genetic testing. As he helped Adrienne navigate the waters of caring for her son with HCM, he simultaneously wanted to research these genes to know if they could be identified, and thus found in me. He wanted to know for my protection if I could potentially develop the disease or one day be a gene carrier who could pass the condition onto my children. At that point in time, the early 2000s, the gene responsible for HCM was not yet identified.

When I became pregnant, the first order of business was to have my half-brother, Marty, genetically tested again. Many new strains of genes that coded for HCM had been identified since my father first began looking into testing in the early 2000s. There are many different markers for the disease, and new medical discoveries are being made all the time. We knew that Marty had a genetic-inheritance component to his condition, so we could only hope that with developments in testing, a marker could be identified.

The geneticist working with my father essentially told him, "Don't waste your time." It was an infinitesimally small chance that one of the newly identified genes would be the one that Marty carried and could be identified. The genetic counselor told him that there was about a 1-percent chance that they'd find an identifiable genetic marker on Marty, as none had been previously discovered. As recently as 2010, only twelve genetic markers for HCM were known. At the time of Marty's testing in 2018, twenty-even markers were known.

Marty went through the straightforward process of doing a buccal swab for the genetic testing. All he had to do was swab the inside of his mouth and send a saliva sample to the lab to be tested. From the start, my father had been in contact with Adrienne, advising her on the process, what to expect, and what we would know when we received the results. We waited five weeks to hear back from the genetics lab. Then, one afternoon in November, I received an email with Marty's test results.

The best-case scenario, the one we were all hoping for, had happened. It was practically a miracle! They had identified the specific HCM gene that runs in our family from testing Marty. Ultimately, this meant that if I was tested and wasn't a gene carrier, our baby would have no chance of inheriting the disease.

A short time after, I completed the same buccal-swab procedure as Marty in order to be tested for the gene. I had a massively high level of anxiety waiting on those test results. I had daily conversations about it with Sean and we came to two conclusions.

God placed me with my parents, Rick and Pam Engelmeier, for a reason. If it turned out that I was a gene carrier and my little boy inherited the disease, I could not possibly be better prepared. We would do everything in our power to ensure that he had the best care and quality of life possible. When HCM is detected and managed early on, people with the disease can have a normal life expectancy. My father has been instrumental in helping Marty receive the best care possible for his condition and in supporting Adrienne and her family through their health-care journey and times of trial. My adoption into the Engelmeier family was bigger than me. It was even bigger than my parents. Because of who my father is, Adrienne's family has had access to top-quality healthcare advice and compassionate support that they might not have received elsewhere. Rick was always working behind the scenes, staying up to date on Marty's condition, conferring with Marty's doctors, and making suggestions where he saw fit. He advocated for Marty in ways that no one else could. My father was always there for Adrienne and her family, before I ever had the chance to reconnect with her. It made it that much easier to transition into a life with Adrienne in it, since a special relationship had already been established between my family and hers.

About a month after I had sent in my sample for evaluation, my father received the results from the genetics lab. It was a Friday night and Sean and I were relaxing at home, enjoying our time together before we became a family of three. I received a text from my mom asking me to call home at my earliest convenience because the results of the genetic testing were in. With shaky hands and a pounding heart, I dialed the number and put it on speakerphone.

Sean could hear it in my dad's voice before I could. I was hoping for the best. Sean, too, was hoping for the best, but was mentally prepared for the worst. My results had come back positive. I had the gene. Our son would have a fifty-fifty chance of inheriting a life-threatening heart condition. And there would be no way to test him until after he was born. We were saddened to hear the news, to say the least. I had a very anxious pregnancy because of it. I prayed every day that God would spare my baby from the awful gene. All we could do was pray and wait.

CHAPTER 18:

~~~

Baby Thomas is Born

My parents had never experienced the birth of a child together. The only births my father witnessed took place during his medical-school days, when he had to stitch up episiotomy victims. I intentionally use the word victim, because who in their right mind lets the doctors in training practice their stitches on such a delicate and important procedure?

My mother was an only child, so she never experienced the birth of a niece or nephew, as many women do if they support a sister through childbirth. She used to tell me that I didn't grow in her belly, I grew in her heart.

As the months of my pregnancy ticked by, I began to consider my birth plan. I knew I wanted Sean to be there for every moment, but I had to ask myself, "Who else do I want in the room, if anyone?"

I came to the conclusion that I wanted to ask my mother to be there. She raised me with all of the love in her being, and I wanted to share this special moment with her. I wanted her and my father to come for the birth, but I initially only wanted my mom and Sean in the delivery room. When I asked her if she'd consider being a support person for me throughout childbirth, she was so touched that she cried. And then I cried, because hormones. And it was a beautiful moment of life coming full circle. She hadn't been able to physically have children of her own, but now her daughter was going to bring a new life into the world, and she was going to be a part of that process.

Thomas was due to arrive on April 6, 2019. My fantastic doctor was scheduled to take a weeklong vacation beginning on his due date. Naturally, I was worried about my first time giving birth, and I wanted to avoid any extra stress. The prospect of having a different doctor at Thomas's birth from the one I'd spent months building a trusting relationship with was something I was not at all fond of. I begged my doctor to induce me if it seemed like I wouldn't be going into labor before Thomas' due date. She wasn't keen on the idea of induction, but assured me that she could sweep the membranes if it didn't seem like he was well on his way by the week before he was due. For those of you who haven't experienced a membrane sweep … it's painful and not at all fun. Google it if you need to know more.

Eight days before my due date, my dilation still hadn't progressed beyond one centimeter. My doctor performed the membrane sweep in hopes of setting labor into motion naturally within the following forty-eight hours or so. It was a Friday afternoon. I spent the rest of that day walking at an outdoor mall near our apartment, stocking up on last-minute items for the baby. The next day, I spent most of my Saturday going up and down four flights of stairs to do laundry at our apartment complex. The women I knew who had endured a membrane sweep told me to keep moving to help things progress, so I did.

Saturday night came and I didn't have so much as a Braxton-Hicks contraction to show for the painful procedure. I had resigned myself to the fact that my baby was going to come on his own time and there was nothing I could do to change that. Sean came home from work, and I made tacos and guacamole for dinner. We sat around enjoying our meal and watching a movie. We were both sleepy and we were getting ready for bed around eleven p.m. when I felt some pains beginning. At first, they felt similar to other discomforts I had experienced throughout my pregnancy, and I didn't think twice about them. But slowly, they began to become rhythmic and undeniable. I was in labor!

After calling my doctor, I called my parents. It was after midnight by this point. My dad answered the phone.

He groggily said, "Hello?"

"Dad, it's me. It's beginning. The contractions started about an hour ago. The doctor said to head into the hospital once they're five minutes apart. You and Mom should start getting ready."

There was a long, vacant pause.

"Dad?"

"Okay," was all he said. It was evident that he was still half-asleep.

"Let me talk to Mom."

I repeated what I had told my father.

My mother squealed, "Oh, Rick! We're about to have a grandbaby!"

My mom immediately kicked things into high gear. My parents had a three-hour drive ahead of them, so she readied the troops and got everyone out the door as quickly as possible.

My parents arrived at the hospital around seven in the morning. At that point, I had already had my epidural and I was laboring comfortably in our birthing suite. Sean was religious about keeping me at ease. He made countless trips to the labor-and-delivery lounge for ice water and popsicles.

I'm pretty sure my mother and I could spend the rest of our lives in conversation given the time, so we spent the next few hours chatting about anything and everything. Sean never left my side. My dad was in and out of the room to walk the family dog, which was waiting in the vehicle through-out the whole ordeal, and he spent a considerable amount of the afternoon napping in the birthing suite's armchair.

Every time my dad left the room, I felt an intense longing to have him back in my space. His calm and competent demeanor in any medical situation gave me confidence and strength. He was always my protector, and I felt the quiet strength of his presence as strongly as ever in my vulnerable time of laboring.

It was about one-thirty in the afternoon when I was getting close to being ready to push. The nurses were busy setting up the suite for delivery when, all of a sudden, I felt the feeling rushing back into my lower body, starting with my feet. One leg began to tingle, and then the other. Before I knew it, it seemed as if I hadn't even been given an epidural at all. The nurse was called in. I could barely speak between contractions and Sean explained to her what was happening. She remained calm, but it was obvious by her urgency that it was going to be a close call to get anesthesia back into the room and get me resituated with an epidural adjustment before delivery.

I had known from the start that I wanted a medicated childbirth. I am not one for pain. Those fifteen minutes before the anesthetist came back to our birthing suite were the longest fifteen minutes of my life. I truly didn't know if I'd have to birth my baby *au naturel* or if I'd benefit from the modern medicine I had always planned on receiving. This was the only time during my birthing experience that I felt scared. My mom kept me going by reading me words of encouragement from a slew of affirmation cards I had created prior to the big day. Thankfully, the anesthetist made it back into the room just in time and adjusted the epidural. It was just the right amount so that I could still feel the pressure of the contractions, but I wasn't suffering from the pain full-force.

I had back labor throughout the process. Thomas was what you call sunny-side up, which means that his face was upward and his little feet were pushing on my spine with every contraction. The typical presentation for a baby is face down. This makes for a much easier birthing experience for both baby and mom. The epidural was a godsend for a situation like mine.

When the time came to push, I remembered the mantra from one of my affirmation cards: "My baby and I are working together." By working together, Thomas and I were able to turn him into the cephalic, or head-down position with my pushes alone. After an hour and twenty minutes of pushing, he made his grand entrance into the world!

With each push, I reminded myself that I was one step closer to meeting my baby. My support team was made up of the absolute best people I could have had by my side. Sean kept me strong with his love. My mom reminded me of the miracle that was taking place in that moment with her gentleness and encouragement. My dad soothed my fears and used his medical expertise to help me figure out how to push in a way that was most effective for the baby and I. The two most important men in my life were just as vital to my birthing success as my mother. My mom was so excited that she gasped happily every time Thomas crowned and she could see his dark hair. Eventually I had to tell her to rein it in because her excitement kept misleading me, making me think I was close to the end.

The epidural must not have been working correctly, because by the final push I fully felt what mothers describe as the ring of fire, when your body is pushed to its absolute limit in the final moments before your baby arrives into the world. The instant I heard Thomas's first cry, though, I forgot all the pain and I broke into a happy sob of elation. "My baby! Oh, my baby!"

I read a novel once where the main character had been separated from her family due to the horrors of war. At the end of the novel, she is reunited with them. Even though decades had passed since they had seen each other, she and her family members still felt the same love they had shared in the past. The description of her emotions in that moment reminded me of what I felt when Thomas was born. The feeling of seeing and hearing and touching my baby for the first time was like meeting a loved one you had always known but had been separated from in another life. It was a blissfully sweet moment of overwhelming joy.

After a few moments, the nurses placed him on my chest. My parents faded into the background and Sean and I marveled at the tiny piece of heaven that we had created. Thomas looked deeply into my eyes, and then his father's, taking it all in. I saw tears glimmer in Sean's eyes as Thomas looked at him for the first time.

I will never forget the birth of my beautiful son. I wish I could go back in time and relive that day. Thomas's birth has brought so much joy to so many.

When I celebrated my first Mother's Day, my own mom gave me the most touching, heartfelt Mother's Day card. Her personal handwritten message on the inside of the beautiful card read,

I will always cherish your beautiful gift of letting me experience your pregnancy, delivery, and caring for little Thomas. I will never forget the wonder of his birth. It was absolutely the most amazing thing I have ever witnessed, and I will cherish it for the rest of my life. Thank you so much for letting me be a part of it with you. I can't wait to see what new adventures and memories we will make in the future! I even get to see what it's like to raise a little boy! Way more blessings than I ever hoped or dreamed!

All my Love,
Mom

When Thomas was less than a week old, we were able to have him tested for the HCM gene. We took our tiny baby boy into the pediatrician's office and the nurse performed the same buccal swab on the inside of his cheeks that Marty and I had done. We had to wait about two weeks for the results.

Again, the results were sent to my father first since he was the cardiologist overseeing the testing. My parents called us at home.

"Lori, it's Dad. I have the test results for Thomas here."

Again, Sean heard it in my father's voice before I did.

"He's negative. He doesn't have the gene, and he will never develop cardiomyopathy."

Tears of joy and relief streamed down my face. Sean beamed from ear to ear. Once you become a parent, there is absolutely nothing in this world more important than the health and well-being of your child. The enormous burden of worry had been lifted from our shoulders. We could finally breathe a sigh of relief. Our little Thomas was the first in three generations to beat the gene.

CHAPTER 19:

≺≺≺

The Melting Pot

PAM AND RICK HAVE BEEN nothing but supportive of my relationship with my biological families. I realize how lucky that makes me. Some parents might feel betrayed or threatened by their child's desire for a relationship with parents who didn't raise them. As a parent myself, I can understand that point of view. But as an adopted person, I know how important it is to have the opportunity to put together the pieces of your identity.

My mother has joyfully encouraged my relationships with both Todd and Adrienne, as well as their families, and she sees these relationships for the blessings they are. My dad had a harder time accepting my relationship with Todd at first. After all, Rick put in the work, love, and time of raising me to adulthood. But over time, as he realized how much my biological family meant to me, he let his guard down. He gets it now. Initially, he just didn't realize how important it was to me to discover where I came from.

You might be reading this and wondering, *What's so important about finding your birth parents? They didn't raise you. They have no stake in who you are. Why would you feel the need to know them?* Only one person has asked me this rude, but well-intentioned, question in my life, yet it made an impression. It made me consider the fact that not everyone can easily understand and accept the life experience of an adopted person.

Pause for just a moment and try to recall any of the advertising you might have seen for services that claim to provide you with extensive knowledge of your heritage or genetic background. I can think of at least three of these types of companies without even looking it up. There are family-tree websites, databases of immigration records, and even genetic tests to determine your biological traits. Why are these so popular? After all, what should it matter where we come from as long as we know who raised us? Right? Wrong.

It is human nature to seek connection to our past so that we can either embrace it or learn from it. The past isn't a place one should live, but a guidepost. Can you imagine how much stronger this desire to know about your background is when you've never even met the very people who gave you life? It does not matter if you had the most picture-perfect upbringing possible, as I did. There is still a part of you that wishes you could put together all the pieces of the puzzle that make you whole.

If you are reading this and you are an adoptive parent, please hear me out. Please do not chastise your child for having a desire to know where they came from. Their interest in their birth family is in no way a reflection of their loyalty or disloyalty to you. They will always love you beyond words, and if they do eventually find and reconnect with their birth parent(s), it will not change how they see you. You will forever be Mom and Dad. The only advice I feel that I can give is to let your child make their own decisions about how they want to handle relationships with their biological family once they are over the age of eighteen. I personally feel that involving a birth parent who has not been involved from the beginning will cause too much conflict in a developing child's life if they are introduced before the child is of an age to begin to understand the situation.

When I first reconnected with my birth parents, I had a hard time navigating those newfound relationships, even as an adult in her twenties. Imagine the havoc it could cause in a child's world if they suddenly needed to try and make sense of a similar situation. It is never a one-size-fits-all solution for anyone, but I think it is important to consider the situation from all angles before opening up the new dimensions of an adopted child's life to them.

There may be instances where a birth parent has been involved from the beginning. In my opinion, this is preferable to introducing a birth parent when the child is older. If the child has grown up with the relationship from the beginning, their world won't be rocked by the sudden introduction of a new family member. But each family has to do what is right for them. I speak only from my perspective as an adopted person and a licensed child-development professional. During my time as a public school teacher in the inner city of Milwaukee, I saw plenty of instances of adoption gone wrong, and many cases where birth parents were reintroduced to a child's life only to turn their world completely upside down.

I also understand that not every adopted person is fortunate enough to have birth parents who went on to have healthy, successful lives like mine did. Some adopted children may have been removed from their birth parent(s) for a number of reasons. Others might come from a situation where their birth mother doesn't know who their birth father is. Still others might come from a birth family with substance-abuse or other significant problems that prevented the parents from keeping and raising their child. I ask adoptive parents, whatever the case may be, please don't stop your child from seeking out their birth family once they have reached adulthood. Even if you know that your child's birth father is a convicted felon serving time in prison or their birth mother is a drug addict who still uses and can't hold a job, let them seek out their biological family and come to their own conclusions. If any of these undesirable factors are the case for your child's birth family, you or another trusted adult could offer to be present when they go to meet them for the first time. No matter what your child decides to do, let your love for them influence your reaction. Support them in their choice, even if it is extremely difficult for you. Remember, it's not about you. It's about your child self-actualizing and reaching the parts of themselves that they have not yet had the chance to discover. Don't we all want that outcome for our children?

CHAPTER 20:

❧

The God who Exceeds Expectations

WHEN I WAS A CHILD, I imagined that meeting my birth parents would go something like this:

> I drive up to my birth mother's house in a nice SUV. I ring the doorbell, and she takes me into her arms, telling me how she has missed me all these years. I come into her home and we talk for hours about my life, my family, my career, and everything that has transpired in her life since I was born. We quickly become the best of friends and, as our relationship grows, I introduce her to my husband, family, and children.

The way that things transpired in real life was not what I imagined. It was more than I ever could have imagined for myself. First of all, I had always thought I'd meet my birth mother before my birth father. It was Adrienne who had sent the most letters and seemed the most interested in me. I knew a lot about her family and her life. I wanted to seek her out and then decide about finding my birth father if it went well with my birth mother. Most adoptees hold a special place in their heart, reserved for the woman who brought them into the world. She holds a kind of mystical power, and they believe that reconnecting with her will fill a place in their soul that has been empty their whole lives.

Only God could have orchestrated such a beautiful beginning to my relationship with my birth families. He gave me the Christmas gift of a lifetime. I walked into that Christmas Eve church service as an only child, and I walked out with two sisters and another set of parents, so to speak, who desperately wanted to include me in their lives! When I came to church that night, I was a mess. I needed a spiritual boost, and my Heavenly Father gave it to me in the form of a family to love, a family that had always been a part of me. They were tucked away like a precious gift a parent holds onto for a child's milestone birthday. A family heirloom, it sits on a shelf or tucked away in a jewelry box for years, and is only passed on when the child is ready to receive it.

Well, let me tell you, I did not feel ready for such a gift on that Christmas Eve of 2010, but God knew it was time. The relationships I started to build with Todd and his family settled a sea of spiritual turmoil and helped me navigate my twenties with more power and grace than I ever would have had on my own.

My parents tried for eight years to have a biological child. They even tried to adopt a child once before me. All of the arrangements had been made. Then, the birth mother changed her mind at the last minute. My parents were heartbroken.

When I was born and Adrienne wanted more time to make her final decision, Mom and Dad were half-expecting their dreams of having a family to be shattered yet again, permanently. My dad even told my mom that if it fell through this time, they were done. He couldn't go through the heartache again, and he definitely couldn't helplessly watch my mom experience it yet another time. Obviously, it didn't come down to that.

Adrienne's life didn't turn out as she planned, of that I am sure. But through my adoption, I would venture to say that it turned out better than she could have imagined. Not only did she find a suitable home for her daughter, but unbeknownst to her at the time, the man she chose to raise her child would also be the man who advocated for her family for years to come. My father's involvement helped to keep Adrienne and her family healthy and he was a sounding board over the years for various medical situations involving Adrienne and her boys. Were it not for him, Marty's HCM might not have been detected early enough. My father pushed for an additional screening when the other cardiologist chalked up Marty's echocardiogram abnormalities to normal variations seen in adolescence. God exceeded Adrienne's expectations, not only in finding a loving home for her daughter but even in supporting her ability to care for her future sons. If it weren't for my father's guidance, Marty's life could have turned out very differently, had the heart condition not been detected early on.

God went above and beyond our expectations for our family. We conceived Thomas on the first try. We had thought it might take months or longer, as it did for most couples we knew. But, we were apparently very fertile and very lucky. During our pregnancy, when we found out we could test for the HCM gene, we had little hope that our specific gene would be identified. We were told that there was a 99-percent chance that we wouldn't find it. Lo and behold, we did! Once we knew that a specific gene that could be identified by a genetic marker ran in our family, others could be tested. It turns out that my brother Ben has the same gene, but is completely asymptomatic. It just goes to show how varied and complex this disease is. Two brothers with the same exact parents and the same exact gene have been affected in vastly different ways. Marty began showing symptoms as a middle-school boy and had a defibrillator surgically placed when he was in high school. Ben is twenty-six, has been monitored his whole life, and has never had a single symptom.

The gene is highly unpredictable. It manifests differently depending on the individual, and there's no way to predict how or when a person will start showing symptoms. All you can do is be vigilant with monitoring.

Once we found out that Thomas was a boy and we knew the risk of passing the gene to him, we almost fully expected him to have it. My biological grandmother passed the gene to all of her children. Her two sons died of the heart condition while her daughter (my birth mother) inherited genetic-carrier status. My birth mother's sons both inherited the gene, while I inherited genetic carrier status from her. The situation was not looking promising, as everyone in the past three generations was either a carrier or had the genetic heart condition themselves. It went against the odds that so many people in one family could all carry the same gene, but it seemed that it was a 100-percent transmission rate. When we found out that Thomas was negative, that he didn't have the gene, and never would, we cried tears of joy, just as we had cried tears of fear and sadness when we found out that I was a gene carrier.

Thomas is our little miracle baby who beat the odds. My brother Marty lovingly nicknamed him, "The Chosen One." All I can do is be forever grateful to God that he gave me a healthy child when all the odds seemed to be stacked against us.

Last, but most certainly not least, God exceeded my expectations for a husband. Only when I finally rested on my faith in His goodness and stopped trying to control the outcomes of my life did He bring me the desire of my heart. The beauty of it is that it was all wrapped up in His perfect plan. Had I not met Todd on Christmas Eve, I never would have been a nanny for the Mellenbergers, Todd's cousin's family. Had I not been their nanny that summer, I never would have met their neighbors who insisted on setting me up on a blind date with Sean.

Sean is more than I could have imagined or hoped for in a husband. He is everything I ever wanted and didn't even know I needed.

As vapid as it sounds, I always saw myself ending up with a preppy white boy. Sean is not at all that stereotype. He is an easygoing man of Lebanese heritage, who darkens to a deep tan in the summer and is often mistaken for Hispanic. His wardrobe has improved over the years with my help, but when I met him he needed a boost in the style department. I saw the diamond in the rough, so to speak. Before Sean, I imagined myself with a doctor, lawyer, or someone of the white-collar type. As the owner of his own tree-service company, Sean is a hardworking business owner who puts a roof over our heads by the sweat of his brow. When I was younger, I always imagined myself with someone who never challenged my point of view and agreed with everything I had to say. Sean is not afraid to tell me when he thinks I'm wrong, and why. He has even changed my mind once or twice in the course of our discussions. Believe me, this is no small feat!

He is at once charming and sincere, opinionated and understanding, strong and assertive, yet gentle and sweet. God knew what I needed in a partner more than I ever did. When Sean came into my life, I honestly went on that first date so that the friends who set us up would quit nagging me to go out with him. Then, once I saw Sean in person and got to know him, I started to fall in love. Neither of us expected anything to come from one blind date, but we have been together ever since. Sean was like a dress at the store that you bypass because you think it will only look good on the hanger, not on you. Then you try it on and it's the perfect fit, and you cannot imagine why you never tried anything like it sooner. He's been my rock of ages and the best father to our children. God's plans are good. All the time, God is good.

Given all of these blessings, I was completely taken aback when, in April of 2021, our son Thomas was diagnosed with leukemia shortly after his second birthday. Our daughter was barely three months old, and we had just been adjusting to and enjoying life as a family of four. Since our daughter was born during the COVID-19 pandemic, we had been relatively strict about visitors until she was out of her most vulnerable time period, the first three months.

Todd and Jamie came to visit us a week before Easter in 2021. We spent quality time with the kids playing at home, and we took them to one of Thomas' favorite playgrounds. The whole weekend, Thomas did not seem like himself. He didn't want to run and play with Todd at the playground. He didn't want to eat any of the special treats Jamie offered him. He was lethargic and not as spunky as everyone knows him to be. Despite his lower energy, he still had bruises from playing even though he hadn't been nearly as active as usual. Jamie and Todd noticed this shift in him, and I casually mentioned that our pediatrician had recommended getting some routine blood work done when we were at his two-year-old checkup the previous week, to rule out anything serious. Jamie and Todd paled when I mentioned this. Todd has a cousin whose firstborn son died from leukemia at a young age, and later, their second born child was diagnosed with leukemia at four years old. It seemed like there was a genetic component of cancer running in the family. We spent the rest of the weekend keeping tabs on Thomas, and he fluctuated between almost normal and back to worn down and not wanting to eat anything. Before Todd and Jamie left to go home, Jamie begged me to get Thomas in for blood work as soon as possible, so that we could all put the worry of our worst fear to rest. I agreed that I would, but I put it off all week, not wanting to face the hassle of dragging two little children into the hospital lab for something that seemed so unnecessary. Deep down, I was absolutely terrified that the beast of cancer was going to make its way back into my life via my precious son.

On Easter Sunday, everything changed. Thomas complained of pain in his legs from simply walking up and down the stairs. He had to be majorly coaxed to search for any of his Easter candy hidden throughout the yard, and he barely ate any of it. Just lifting the candy to his mouth seemed to hurt him. We gave him a bath, and he cried in pain when being washed in the groin area or being lifted under his arms. When he spiked a fever of one hundred and one, we knew something was definitely wrong. We took him into urgent care, and the doctor on call looked him over and recommended rest and fluids as well as taking Thomas in for lab work the following day. Since it was a holiday weekend, no one was available that day to do the blood work.

I took Thomas in for the blood work in the morning, and we spent the rest of the day doing normal activities like playing outside and playing in his playroom. By lunchtime, it was clear to me that Thomas was completely exhausted. I knew something had to be seriously wrong. He didn't have a fever, but he was not the whirling dervish I knew to be my son.

I had to work at my job as a dance instructor that night, and I poured myself into teaching my classes to try to distract my mind from the gnawing worry I felt for my son. I hammed it up for my two- and three-year-old classes, being extra energetic and silly with them. Then, I worked my strength and conditioning students hard, cheering them on and doing most of the exercises alongside them. At the end of my strength and conditioning class, I was preparing to teach three more classes for the night when my boss and one of my coworkers came into the studio.

"Miss Lori," my coworker Emma said calmly, "Your husband is on the phone. It's regarding Thomas." I knew in my gut that my fear had been realized. I gasped, struggling to catch my breath, and my boss, Kate, gently put her hands on my shoulders. Looking me in the eyes, she said,

"We got this. Everything's going to be okay. You get home to your baby."

I ran to the front desk to take the call from Sean.

"Sean?" I asked. "What is it? Are the kids okay?" I was internally shaking, and I felt like I could just about jump out of my skin.

"Yeah, everything's fine," he said. "But the doctor's office called, and they said they want us to take him into the Emergency Room at Children's because of some abnormal things in his blood work."

My world stopped spinning. I grabbed my keys and sprinted out of the dance studio, driving as fast as I possibly could without getting pulled over. When I walked through the front door, Sean was packing up both children to get us to the hospital.

"I didn't want to tell you this over the phone," Sean said. "But the doctor said that what they saw in his blood work could be indicative of leukemia. Nothing is for sure yet, but she wants us to get him in right away. And hon, if that's what this is, we're going to fight it, and the doctor said we caught it early if it is." I broke out into sobs. I couldn't believe my ears. Yet, I had the presence of mind to pack the diaper bag and some snacks for Thomas while Sean got the kids situated in the car. I was blinded by tears, but I was also in high-gear survival mode. As a mother, you have to swallow the fear and lean into the survival instincts in times of crisis.

We called Todd and Jamie on our drive to the hospital. Jamie answered.

"It's Lori and Sean," I said, my voice breaking. She knew we'd gone in for the blood work earlier that day. "We . . ." I choked up and couldn't get a word out.

"What is it, my girl?" Jamie asked, concern heavy in her voice.

Sean took over the phone call and told Todd and Jamie what was happening. "We'll keep you guys posted. And thank you for pushing us to get him in. Whatever this is, we're going to find it and nip it in the bud. And we're finding it that much sooner because of you."

From the time of our initial visit to the Emergency Department at Children's Hospital of Wisconsin to the end of Thomas' first admission, it was a total of thirty-five days spent in the hospital. Thomas went right into the oncology unit the night we brought him to the emergency room, and he started chemo a few days later. What started out as some abnormal blood work turned into a month-long hospital stay. It was traumatic to say the least. Our family was immediately torn in two, trying to figure out how to manage a newborn, a child with a serious medical diagnosis in the hospital, and keeping Sean's business, our main income, afloat. What followed that first admission for treatments was six grueling months of chemotherapy for Thomas. We spent a month at a time in the hospital with a week or less at home in between treatments. Sean's parents and my parents went above and beyond to help us. Our mothers took turns staying at our home and keeping things running while caring for our infant daughter. They brought her to the hospital every day so that I could still spend time with her and continue to nurse her, even though I wasn't at home. Sean and I made sure that one of us was always present with Thomas at the hospital. This meant that Sean worked during the week, and I lived at the hospital Monday through Friday, while Sean stayed with Thomas on the weekends. Most nights, Sean came to the hospital after working all day to see Thomas and me. We could not have kept this up without the help of our family.

Another amazing way that our family came through for us was in the way that Adrienne and my entire biological family supported us. As I mentioned earlier, Adrienne has vast experience with event planning. She has helped plan and execute countless benefits, fundraisers, and social events over the years. Shortly after Thomas was diagnosed, she asked my permission to host a benefit for Thomas and our family. She planned the biggest and most successful benefit that central Wisconsin has ever seen! Because of her hard work, our family did not have to struggle financially when Sean lost weeks of work to be present at the hospital. We were able to make a big dent in the medical costs that six months of inpatient cancer treatments incur. From a horrible situation, a lot of people were brought together in love. Adrienne, Daryl, Todd, Jamie, my sisters, my brothers, my biological cousin Casie, and dozens of other friends and even total strangers worked hard to plan the benefit, staff the different events of the day, and make sure it all ran smoothly. At the benefit itself, Adrienne and my dad had a chance to sit and have a long talk. The same happened separately for my dad and Todd. It was especially wonderful to witness my dad and Todd having a one-on-one conversation. My dad stepped out of his comfort zone to be at the event in the first place, as big gatherings are not his thing. Then, to see him conversing with my birthfather was above and beyond anything I'd hoped for the day. Their relationship was not strained in the past; they just didn't have much of one. It made my heart overflow with love and joy to see the people I love most in the world coming together for the sake of my beloved family.

When Thomas was first diagnosed, I found myself warring with God. Why did He allow my baby to be spared from the cardiomyopathy gene only to have him suffer through Leukemia? Thomas showed no evidence of disease after his first round of treatments, which was a huge blessing. Yet, I still felt angry that this even had to happen in the first place and that for the rest of my life I'd be looking over my shoulder praying that the cancer would never come back.

I started writing updates on social media to share my experience and to keep everyone in the loop on our sweet boy. One of my updates made it much farther than just a computer or smartphone screen. Adrienne's cousin, who is a pastor, decided to share it with her congregation as part of her sermon. In my opinion, this was another example of the divine in the everyday. Somehow, through my suffering, I was able to reach out and help others. Were it not for my willingness to be vulnerable and my connection with Adrienne, that message wouldn't have reached that congregation, and maybe, just maybe, there was someone there who really needed to hear it. Here is what I had to say:

Alright, folks. Since it's Sunday I thought I'd share some thoughts I've had about faith since this whole journey began.

The day of Thomas's diagnosis, I was so mad at God. Like, furious. And I didn't want to be. God has been such a rock and has brought so much good together for my life. I just didn't understand how He could allow this to happen to Thomas, especially after Thomas had been spared from a genetic heart defect. The first in three generations to be spared, by the way! I expressed my feelings to my good friend, who is also Thomas's godmother. She told me that it's okay to be mad at God. She told me faith is a relationship, and in any relationship you will get upset with the other person at some point. The way to address it is to express it. She told me that God can take it. That really clicked with me.

So, I decided to let God have it. I yelled at Him for a few days. I sobbed it out in the shower. I kept asking why. Over, and over, and over again. But, I also thanked Him. I thanked Him for the blessings of my family and friends who have supported us every step of the way. I thanked Him for both of my beautiful babies. I thanked Him for the love of my life, my rock solid husband. And I prayed and continue to pray with all my heart that Thomas will be healed if it is His divine will. Another friend told me that God loves Thomas even more than I do. He wouldn't allow this to happen to Thomas without a greater plan. That sounds so barf-worthily clichéd, but I do believe it to be true.

So, now, I am leaning on my faith more than ever. And I have seen nothing but good because of it. The news just keeps getting better and better. I finally feel hopeful. No matter how this turns out, I know that God has our back. And I do believe that Thomas will kick this cancer to the curb and one day this will all be a distant memory. Now is my time to step up to the plate and live my faith by trusting in God. I'm praying that this journey will allow me to witness in ways I never have before. God is great. And love is bigger than fear.

Romans 5:3–4 NIV

"… but we also glory in our sufferings, because we know that suffering produces perseverance; perseverance, character; and character, hope."

CHAPTER 21:

Presence

PRESENCE IS ALL IT TAKES to make a difference. My acceptance of the people who have entered my life via my biological family has been a huge blessing for me and for many others. Opening myself to the love of my biological family helped me to grow as a person and brought joy to the lives of my birth parents, their families, and many friends whom I have come to know and love.

I believe that the purpose of life is to love deeply and fully. God is love. The more love we share, the more we receive. The more we love, the more connected we are to God and the universe. Love is divine, and it is powerful. We spend our whole lives learning how to give and receive love. It is a skill we are put on this earth to attempt to master.

I thought I knew what love was. Then I became a mother. There are days my heart is so full of love that I think it might burst. I look at my son and daughter and I tear up with joy. My little miracle baby beat the odds of inheriting the familial heart condition. The chosen one. He has blessed me beyond measure. He helps me to see the world through new eyes. He brings me into the present moment to experience the gift of sharing it with him. The miracle of my pregnancy and bringing him into this world shattered walls in my heart that I didn't even know existed. There are days I feel so deeply connected to God and all that is good in the world, it's as if all of the positive energy in the universe is pulsating through me and radiating outward, because of this love for my children. My husband and I were merely the vehicle for God to bring our little angels into the world. He did the rest.

Then there is my daughter, Verna. She was born in the midst of a worldwide pandemic. She was conceived at a time when the world was an uncertain mess. Yet, God knew she had to be a part of our family. She is a radiant little starburst of joy. Her early days were different than I ever imagined they would be. With her brother in the hospital for a month at a time receiving cancer treatments, I had to get creative to find ways to spend time with her each day, and still be there for my son so that my husband could work. My daughter had to adapt quickly to new caregivers in her life. A silver lining of Thomas's diagnosis was that Verna had the chance to spend lots of one-on-one time with her grandparents, who truly uprooted their lives to care for her. My mom and Sean's mom took on the brunt of her care while we were inpatient with Thomas, bringing her to the hospital every day so that I could see her. My relationship with Verna stayed strong despite all of the challenges we faced in her first year. I am forever grateful for the gift of my wonderful, supportive family, and the gift of my babies.

In 2019, we traveled up to Houghton, Michigan, for a family reunion. Thomas was a mere four months old at the time. I held him on my hip in Grandma Williams' kitchen as she gushed over his sweet smile. She said to me:

> "It's so good that you bring him (Thomas) around the family. You're so generous with him, and he can feel that love and sense of belonging. Even now, he knows how loved he is. It's so important for children to have a place where they belong. When they don't, they turn to other things like gangs or violence. And we saw some of that in our travels, living all over the globe. The children who aren't supported and loved at home will go elsewhere to find it. You're doing such a great service to him by helping him become part of a family social group at such a young age."

Grandma Williams and her husband raised five children together. All of their grown children are as different as different can be, but they all turned out to be wonderful people. She made the world a better place by raising her children right, and she is a reminder that I am changing the world one little heartbeat at a time as I pour myself into my children.

When I was a student teacher, I worked in an English as a Second Language (ESL) classroom for part of my certification. I had the privilege to teach ESL to students from all over the world. Part of this experience involved a special project with a diverse group of fifth-grade girls. My mentor teacher was the supervisor for their project. As such, I was automatically a mentor for them as well. I may have even taken over a little bit because the girls related more to me than they did my hilarious but older male counterpart.

As the topic of their presentation, all of the fifth graders were to choose something that they believed could affect their community and the world for the better. Some students' projects focused on ways to live a more eco-friendly lifestyle. Others initiated a project to start urban community gardens. My girls chose the topic of gang membership. They delved into the root causes of why youth become involved in criminal gangs. It was a bold topic of choice for these young ladies to immerse themselves in.

In the Midwest, gangs are primarily made up of minorities. Often, refugee and immigrant youths who don't have a specific niche in society are the exact people targeted by gangs for membership. Gang members know that these young people yearn for a sense of belonging and they know that they can provide it for them. Some of the girls in my fifth grade-project group knew people personally who were involved in gangs or affected by gang violence. This was especially true for the ESL students of the group, who had seen brothers or cousins or uncles involved with gangs or affected by gang violence.

As part of their project, the girls wanted to interview a former gang member. Can you imagine that? A group of eleven-year-old girls matter-of-factly deciding that they wanted an audience with a former violent criminal! They are certainly braver than I was at their age, and I am exceedingly proud of them to this day. I hope they know that.

Enter Jose Vasquez. Mr. Vasquez grew up on the south side of Milwaukee in an impoverished Hispanic neighborhood. In his own words,

> "I was part of a gang by the time I was seven years old. I didn't
> know it. All I knew is that it was my family. All the guys around
> me were involved with the gang. I had no father around and an
> abusive mom at home, so I didn't really feel a sense of safety or
> belonging anywhere. I would run with these kids and teens in
> the streets and they were all involved with the gang somehow.
> So I just knew it as my life and I accepted it as a fact from day
> one that I would be in the gang too."

Jose paid the price for his involvement with the gang. He was shot six times by a rival gang member and survived, but he ended up in prison as a consequence of his actions. During his incarceration, he had a major change of heart and decided that he wanted to make the world a better place by helping to keep kids out of gangs and off the streets. He started a non-profit group in Milwaukee that is focused on mentoring youth in his former neighborhood. The Clarke Square Neighborhood Initiative provides work permits and housing resources, job-prep programs, wellness and arts programs, and, most importantly, love and compassion without judgment.

I believe I was meant to be in that classroom with those brave young ladies as their mentor so that I could in turn learn from their experience with Mr. Vasquez. His story underpinned the importance of family and belonging as I had never known before. I knew that, because of his story, I needed to share mine. I can only hope that my story helps others, too.

I am a vessel shaped by the love of four families. I am my roots, and I am my raising. I am a person who is finally comfortable in her own skin. I am proud of the woman I am today because I went through a hell of a time becoming her. I am a lover, a mother, a friend, a daughter, a wife, and a teacher. I am a powerful woman. I am who I am because I have made the conscious choice to peel back the layers of myself that were buried for years.

This is my story, as an adopted person who has reconnected with her biological family. I hope that, in its own way, it helps you.

Your life is just that. Yours. You hold the pen and write your own story every day. You have the power to make it beautiful.

FAQs/Comments about Adoption and How to Handle Them

1. **Using any form of the phrase "your real parents" to describe biological parents.**

    My parents who raised me are my real parents. Last time I checked, the fact that I didn't enter this world via my adopted mother's womb never influenced the realness of her motherhood. My mom and dad put in the years of hard work, joy, and heartache to raise me. They are Mom and Dad, and they always will be. Please do not ever refer to an adopted person's biological parents as their real parents. It devalues the relationship they have with their own family and gives their adoptive parents no credit. It is better to use the term biological parents or birth parents out of respect. As I have mentioned before, Pam and Rick raised me to adulthood. Adrienne and Todd raised me through it. My adoptive parents laid the foundation of who I am, and my birth parents helped me to discover new and deeper facets to my story.

    If you are an adopted person and it bothers you when someone refers to your birth parents as your real parents, just try to see the moment as a chance to educate a person who might not even realize what they are saying. Here is a scripted example to get you started:

    Friend: "Oh, so your real mom and dad were just too young at the time, that's why they put you up for adoption."

Me: "Yes. But I refer to them as my birth parents. My real mom and dad are the parents who raised me since I was a baby."

Say it with a smile on your face and in a genuine tone of voice. The friend you're speaking with probably never considered how their phrasing comes across. You can help them understand how to correctly address the situation.

2. **What about your wedding? Now which dad will walk you down the aisle?**

Yes, someone asked me this at one point in time. Why would there be any question?! The man who raised me to be who I am and who financed the majority of my wedding is absolutely walking me down the aisle.

There are many ways to include biological family in a wedding ceremony. Here is a list of examples of how my birth parents, half siblings, and extended biological family members were involved in mine:

I invited my birth parents, their spouses, and their children (my half-siblings) to the wedding.

I invited my biological grandparents from both sides, as well as biological aunts, uncles, and cousins.

My half-sisters stood up in the wedding party as bridesmaids.

My half-brother was an usher.

My birth mother was an event coordinator, helping to organize all the details of the big day.

My birth father's wife and my half-sisters helped plan and decorate for the wedding shower

My mom crafted a special family tree for the wedding reception. It was a beautiful, white, light-up tree with handmade ornaments featuring the wedding photos of our parents, grandparents, aunts and uncles, and anyone in the generations before ours whose wedding photos we could get our hands on. We included my birth parents as well as biological grandparents on the family tree. This is the tree seen on the cover of this book.

3. **Upon realizing that my mom and birthmother have a friendly relationship, saying to me, "That's just weird!"**

Maybe to you it is. But it is my normal and I am so extremely thankful for it. Point being, if you think my family situation is weird or odd or you couldn't handle it, keep it to yourself.

Take a moment to picture a child of divorced parents. This child has two parents who love her. Mom and Dad stay amicable and occasionally they celebrate milestones or holidays together with their child. This would be ideal for a child of divorce. If this type of situation does exist, no one goes around telling the child how weird it is if their parents get along or how abnormal their lifestyle is. So, don't do it to adopted people either.

4. **"What's the big deal? If you had such a great life, why would you even want to meet your birth parents?"**

The answer to this question circles back to what I have previously explained. Everyone has an innate desire to know who they are. Part of knowing who you are is knowing where you came from. No matter how you feel about it, genetics play an essential role in who we become, to a certain degree.

Imagine this scenario from a medical-history perspective. Can you imagine asking someone who has a family history of cancer and wanted to be tested for a cancer-linked gene, "What's the big deal? You're healthy now. Why would you even want to know?" Their desire to test for the gene is a very personal decision, and it is understandable why someone would choose to do so. When an adopted person wants to reunite with their biological family, it is the same idea. It is their business if they choose to do it. Not anyone else's. And it brings a level of knowledge and under-standing that may be hurtful or helpful, just like the cancer-gene test would. But, if someone is brave enough to seek out that risk, they abso-lutely should not be judged for it.